TO BOLDLY GROW

Also by Tamar Haspel
with Barbara Haspel

The Dreaded Broccoli Cookbook:
A Good-Natured Guide to Healthful Eating with 100 Recipes

TO BOLDLY GROW

Finding Joy, Adventure, and Dinner
in Your Own Backyard

TAMAR HASPEL

G. P. PUTNAM'S SONS

NEW YORK

PUTNAM
— EST. 1838 —

G. P. PUTNAM'S SONS
Publishers Since 1838
An imprint of Penguin Random House LLC
penguinrandomhouse.com

Library of Congress Cataloging-in-Publication Data

Names: Haspel, Tamar, author.
Title: To boldly grow: finding joy, adventure, and dinner in your own backyard / Tamar Haspel.
Identifiers: LCCN 2021054167 (print) | LCCN 2021054168 (ebook) |
ISBN 9780593419533 (hardcover) | ISBN 9780593419540 (ebook)
Subjects: LCSH: Haspel, Tamar. | Subsistence farming—United States—Handbooks,
manuals, etc. | Subsistence fishing—United States—Handbooks, manuals, etc. |
Subsistence hunting—United States—Handbooks, manuals, etc. | Self-reliant living—
United States—Handbooks, manuals, etc. | Women journalists—United States—Biography. |
Gardeners—United States—Biography.
Classification: LCC S501.2 .H37 2022 (print) | LCC S501.2 (ebook) |
DDC 630.973—dc23/eng/20211207
LC record available at https://lccn.loc.gov/2021054167
LC ebook record available at https://lccn.loc.gov/2021054168

Printed in the United States of America
1st Printing

Book design by Laura K. Corless

For my parents,
Barbara and the late Chuck Haspel

Everything important that I know,
I learned at home.

CONTENTS

CONTENTS

PART IV
Foraging

PART V
Turkeys

PART VI
Hunting

THE FIRST FIRST-HAND FOOD

A s a child, I learned exactly one thing about gardening: if you don't much like to garden, mint is the plant for you.

I grew up in a food-focused household, but that focus didn't extend to growing it. Mostly my parents let someone else get the food to the point where you could eat it or cook with it, and they took it from there. For a few years, though, we did have a small garden on the south side of the house, and I have hazy memories of peppers and tomatoes. But I definitely remember the mint, which was positively magic. All you have to do is put a little in the ground once, and it comes up year after year, bigger, brighter, and mintier. The import of this came home to me fully when I was old enough for juleps.

Having a particular affinity for plants that require no care at all didn't exactly set me up for a future getting my dinner with my own two hands. In fact, I spent the first four decades of my life giving almost no thought to where my food came from, let alone the options for rolling up my sleeves and procuring it myself. I had limited and inauspicious experience with gardening, but the other kinds of first-hand food activities—fishing, foraging, hunting—weren't even in shouting distance of anything I was familiar with. My job for most of my adult life was to find interesting things other people were doing and write about them for magazines, which I could do from the comfort and safety of my armchair.

I've never been much of a doer. A reader, all my life. A writer, since about the age of thirty. I've always been curious, engaged, interested—I wanted to know something about everything, so long as no actual effort was involved. Give me a book about, say, octopus intelligence, and I will feel no need to learn to scuba dive. I'm interested in all the things my fellow humans are up to around the world, but I like to find out without worrying about exchange rates or lost luggage. As long as you can modify it with *armchair*, I could be anything.

This isn't a bad worldview for a writer. I couldn't have cut it as a war correspondent, but if you're writing about nutrition and diet and science, an armchair is a fine place to do it from. For many years, I made a perfectly respectable living doing just that for magazines like *Self*, *Glamour*, and *Women's Health*. I learned enough about all those things to be good at my job and also to make people's eyes glaze over at parties, so if you have questions about omega-3 fats or carbohydrate metabolism, I'm here for you.

I'd established a comfortable career by the time I met Kevin. I was thirty-eight and he was forty, and within weeks we knew that we were in for the duration. Within months, we were living together in my Upper West Side Manhattan apartment. We got married on the third anniversary of our first date because that way we'd have to remember only one date (we usually forget anyway). To be fair, by that time I had already figured out that Kevin, unlike me, *was* a doer, so I knew what I was getting into.

But you marry a doer at your peril, because you never know exactly what he's going to want to do.

Kevin, it turned out, wanted to do a garden. And he wanted to do it on the roof of our building.

"Could we have mint?" I asked, first thing. Juleps for everybody!

"No mint," said Kevin. "It takes over everything."

"Isn't that why it's good?"

And that's when I came face-to-face with Kevin's idea of gardening and discovered it was much more robust, much more realistic, much more *active*, than mine. There were no armchairs involved. The things it did involve—heavy lifting, special equipment, regular maintenance—weren't exactly in my wheelhouse. And although I was familiar with dirt, I'd never had to actively acquire it; it seemed to gravitate to me of its own accord.

But as Kevin talked about it, I found that I was curious. I was engaged. I was interested.

And I was in.

A big part of our building's roof was tiled and landscaped and furnished; it was a much-used amenity for the residents. But there was a part accessible only by ladder, home to some mysterious parts of the building's infrastructure, and that's where we wanted to put the garden. To my surprise, when I asked the building manager whether we could keep a few pots up there, she immediately said yes. Even so, I was a little worried.

"What if people see this and then everyone wants to do it?" I asked Kevin. There obviously wasn't room for everyone, so that would put the kibosh on the whole undertaking.

Kevin laughed out loud. "People here don't even cook their own food," he told me. "I guarantee they have no interest in growing it."

Let the doing begin.

Oh wait, not quite yet! I got to ease into this gently because the very first step wasn't doing at all. It was research.

Now, I actually know something about research. And as with all highly technical subjects made more complex by the conflicting opinions of both so-called experts and crank amateurs, there's only one place to go to ferret out the truth. So Kevin and I sat up late into the night, cruising the internet, trying to figure out what would and would not grow in a pot.

I learned that tomatoes were way more complicated than I'd given them credit for. While I'd always categorized them by straightforward characteristics like size, color, and deliciousness, there are other categories that are harder to make sense of. Tomatoes might be determinate or indeterminate. They also might be VFN or open-pollinating.

Yikes.

This is where I balked. We were prepared to spend time, money, and effort establishing a garden on our roof, and I was going into it with absolutely no expertise. And although Kevin had grown tomatoes before, he didn't know what VFN was, either. But he was pretty confident that knowing wasn't a prerequisite for growing tomatoes.

"My father never knew, and he grew great tomatoes," he pointed out.

And, if you think about it, you realize that nearly every backyard gardener grows tomatoes, and we could bet what percent of them know what VFN is. I'd go somewhere in single digits. Yet every summer, gardens reliably produce tomatoes. Sure, there's lots to know about gardening, and there are lots of experts to tell you what those things are. And I'm glad they're out there! I'm sure they're improving the overall field of backyard vegetables! But all you have to do is look around to realize you don't need to know everything they know just so you can have a really delicious BLT.

I shut down the computer, and the next day we took a trip out of the city to the biggest nursery we knew of, where we met Mike, who worked in the vegetable department. We asked him which tomatoes would do well in pots, and he told us to try Celebrity and Sweet 100s. That's what we bought. The peppers would all do fine, he said, so we got some sweet and some hot.

Once we'd settled on tomatoes and peppers, we moved on to the fruit section, where Kevin's one shortcoming as a husband reared its ugly head. I'm not complaining—Kevin is interesting and smart, funny and kind, responsible and considerate, so I'm certainly willing to overlook the fact that blackberries are his favorite fruit.

It's a choice I can't get my mind around. It's not that I dislike black-berries, but it seems to me that the fruit pantheon offers so many bet-ter choices. Mangoes! Cherries! Nectarines! Even raspberries, Kevin's second-favorite fruit, are more understandable. But blackberries have a mysterious hold on Kevin, and so we headed for the blackberry section.

On the way to the blackberries, we passed the mint. I figured I'd give it one last try and stopped to pick up one of the little pots.

"Can we have mint?" But Kevin held firm.

No mint. Blackberries.

Blackberries are different from other plants in that they come up every year. That makes them, I was given to understand, a perennial. Kind of like mint! My spirits brightened, but they were immediately dashed when Kevin explained that yes, they come up every year, but they still require special equipment and regular maintenance. We have to train them to grow up the wall, put nets around them to keep the birds away, prune them down to their stems when the season is over, and carefully preserve them for next year. Sounds like a lot of work just so you can get those little seeds stuck between your teeth. We bought one blackberry and one raspberry plant.

To round out our garden, we chose basil and cilantro, both of which apparently have a shallow root system, to cohabit with the tomatoes.

That ended the plant portion of the program, and we moved on to special equipment.

It started with something in which to plant the plants. Something large. It turned out there's a booming business in large things to put plants in, and we had many choices. I leaned toward plastic pots because they're cheap and light. Kevin leaned toward whiskey barrel halves because they're expensive and heavy. Okay, not *just* because they're expensive and heavy. Also because they will last for many years. Since I thought it was a big hairy deal to commit to a garden for one year, I didn't necessarily see a pot's ten-year lifespan as an asset, but I found myself succumbing to the appeal of Kevin's vision. Whiskey barrels it was.

We had to fill those barrels with something, and I found the idea of buying dirt a little disconcerting. Why should you shell out good money for something that accumulates under your fingernails for free? Two reasons, it turns out: quantity and quality. You don't realize how big whiskey barrels are until you try to wedge them into the back seat of a Saab. Filling them up with what accumulates under your fingernails would take a lifetime. Besides, fingernail dirt is the wrong kind of dirt. Your plants are going to be entirely dependent on the dirt that you give them, so it's best to let a professional make sure it's the right kind. We stocked up on potting mix.

That's when I thought we were done, but Kevin told me there was one more thing we needed. Rocks. Oh, sure, he called it *aggregate*, but I wasn't born yesterday—I know that *aggregate* is a fancy word for rocks. Well, if you're going to buy dirt, you might as well buy rocks. Next thing you know, we'll be buying dust, or maybe lint. I got on the checkout line while Kevin went to find the rock section.

A few minutes later he came back empty-handed. The aggregate was the wrong kind; they only had small rocks, and we needed big rocks. So now what? "Don't worry," said Kevin, and added those four little words that strike fear into spouses everywhere: "I have an idea."

I put my fear on hold while we schlepped our plants, our pots, and our dirt home. Let the heavy lifting commence! We lugged the barrels up to the roof. We hauled the bags of dirt, one at a time, up the ladder. Then Kevin let me in on his idea.

Our apartment was only a couple blocks from the Hudson River, and rivers, as anyone can tell you, are just filled with rocks.

Kevin took our cart—the kind that little old ladies take to the market—and headed for the Hudson. He scrambled down the bank (it was low tide) and collected his rocks. He piled them in the cart and managed, with some effort, to get back up the bank, rocks in tow.

The riverfront is a popular recreation destination, and Kevin's rock hunt had an audience of sunbathers, dog walkers, bike riders, and Saturday-afternoon strollers. What they saw was a wild-haired man in filthy shorts and T-shirt filling a little-old-lady cart with rocks. This was New York, though, and nobody batted an eye. (One of our neighbors evidently spotted us. When we got home, our doorman told us someone had left something for us, then handed us a rock with a Post-it with our apartment number written on it.)

We finally got to the heart of the matter—putting the plants and the rocks and the dirt in the pots. That's the part that I really think of as gardening, and it took about seven minutes.

I had to hand it to him. Our rooftop garden was beautiful, and we visited almost every day to check the progress. While regular maintenance was involved, it was mostly just turning on a hose and plucking out any weeds. Soon the tomatoes got flowers and then promising little green fruits. The cucumber vines spread over the grates that covered the building's skylights, our urban stand-in for trellises. There was visible growth every day, and I started—just started, mind you—to understand why people do this.

And then the tomatoes ripened, and the light went on.

They were the super-sweet little cherry tomatoes, and although I wouldn't testify in a court of law that they were the best tomatoes the world had ever seen, that's what they seemed like. I couldn't tell you whether they were determinate or indeterminate, VFN or open-pollinated. I don't know what was in the special soil. What I can tell you is that we put seedlings in the ground, watered them regularly, and went from zero to tomato in just a few months.

They were the first homegrown food of my adult life, and they took me by surprise.

Yes, the flavor, but more the feeling. I was *invested* in those tomatoes. I had worked for those tomatoes. I was proud of those tomatoes. I didn't know it at the time, but the experience of those tomatoes was going to shape the next chapter of my life.

That chapter began in 2008, when our financial lives, like those of so many others, were beginning to look shaky. The internet was pulling the rug out from under both of our careers. Mine, because magazine publishers were struggling to figure out how to publish online content *and* pay writers. Kevin's, because the commodity trading he did for a living was moving from the physical exchange floor onto a virtual platform. We didn't know whether either of us was going to be able to make another red cent.

The good news, though, was that we could make the attempt from anywhere, and we'd been thinking about Cape Cod for many years. I had spent my childhood summer vacations there, and Kevin and I had aspired to a summerhouse. Since that wasn't in the cards, we had to pick: New York or Cape Cod.

It's not so much we picked Cape Cod as we picked disruption. Since circumstances were wreaking havoc with our lives, why not just go all in and move to a tiny house on two acres of woods in what felt to me like the back of beyond but was really just a long driveway down from a main road, with excellent cell service and town water. I will confess that it was hard to leave New York, which we loved then and still love now. But we wanted to shake things up, so we pulled up our socks and our stakes, and started focusing on things we could do on Cape Cod that we couldn't do in Manhattan.

And I kept thinking about those tomatoes. If there's one thing Cape Cod has over New York, it's first-hand food opportunities. A few months into our residency, I started taking inventory of them, but it was autumn and the pickings were slim. Although, when we moved in, it had been too late to start a proper garden, we did have some collard greens going, and big plans for the next year. And because it was heading into winter, most of the fish had already moved on to more hospitable waters. It had gotten too cold for the wild mushrooms, let alone the berries and beach plums. What Cape Cod has in abundance, though, all year round, is clams.

I bought a used clam rake at an estate sale (only $10, but it had seen better days) and ventured out. I didn't have the foggiest idea what I was doing, and my first foray was an ignominious episode involving wandering around on a beach known to be clamless, on a day when clamming was forbidden, using a clam rake to dig where clams wouldn't be caught dead. So I paid a visit to our town's natural resources department, confessed my cluelessness, and came away with a license ($30), a working knowledge of the rules (Wednesday, Saturday, and Sunday are clamming days), and a hot tip on where clams might actually be (Cotuit Bay).

I remember with vivid distinctness the first clam I raked out of the seabed. It took me a while to find it, and I raked up a lot of rocks, many clamshells, and a mysterious vertebra before I did. But when I pulled the rake out of the water and it had an actual clam in it—cherrystone size—it felt nothing short of miraculous. We live in a world where you can go outside and dig your dinner up out of the sand!

I came home with enough for a meal, and although I wouldn't testify in a court of law that it was the best clam pasta the world had ever seen, that's what it seemed like.

Gardening and clamming, the activities, don't bear much resemblance to each other. One is terrestrial and one, aquatic. One yields a plant, and the other, an animal. The skills and tools involved are completely different. Only one requires waders, which are unflattering to absolutely everybody. But the satisfaction of the food itself was identical. In the next few years, I'd discover it was the same with fish I'd caught, venison I'd hunted, mushrooms I'd foraged. Yet there was no name either for that satisfaction or for the category of food that elicited it. The category, I've taken to calling *first-hand food*. I still don't know what to call the satisfaction beyond satisfaction, but it felt different to me than other kinds.

And that is why, on New Year's Day, 2009, when Kevin and I were coming to grips with not being New Yorkers anymore and trying to find our purpose in this new place, I floated an idea. An idea for a project. A project with a purpose.

"Honey," I said, "do you think we can go a whole year and eat at least one thing every day that we get first-hand? Food that we grow or fish or hunt or gather?"

Kevin is always supportive of me and my work, likes the idea of trying new things, and is possessed of an irrepressible can-do attitude.

"Not a chance," he said.

"Not a chance?" I asked, a bit bewildered. You don't know either of us well enough yet to understand what a dramatic role reversal this was. Kevin is usually the one ready to jump in, give it a go. I am the cautious one who has to read up, to prepare.

"What are we going to eat all winter?" he asked.

I took a mental inventory. Our collard greens had come to fruition, and there were some in the freezer, along with a little parsley and dill. There was some red pepper jelly left over from our Manhattan rooftop garden. I had to admit it didn't look promising.

"I think we could spend this year preparing and do it next year," Kevin said.

"Preparing?" I was a little incredulous. This was not the husband I was accustomed to. "Next you'll be telling me we should read the instructions."

"We won't have anything new until May," he said. That's when we could reasonably start to catch saltwater fish. "And no vegetables until July at the earliest."

"Aren't trout year-round?" I asked. Our house was on a lake that was stocked regularly, and Kevin acknowledged that we'd probably be able to catch some over the winter. "And we'll have mussels, oysters, and clams," I said. "And a few things we have put by," I added, without mentioning that one of them was eleven jars of imperfectly set red pepper jelly.

"That's not very much," Kevin said. Which of course was true. This wasn't going to be easy, especially in the first few months. But I wanted to do it anyway.

And there's that word: *do*. Looking back, I find it hard to put my finger on why this project was compelling enough to get me, the non-doer, out of my armchair. It wasn't because I was opting out of our food system; Kevin and I have never been big consumers of the kinds of processed foods implicated in obesity and disease. It wasn't because we were aiming for self-sufficiency; we're staunch advocates of interdependence.

It was simply the tomatoes. It was the clams. It was the sense of accomplishment, and also the meals, that came from going outside, rolling up my sleeves, and taking a flyer on something I'd never done before, something just a little bit outside my comfort zone. I'd spent the last decade writing about things other people did with food, and it was time to do a little doing myself.

In the end, Kevin wasn't that hard to convince. He likes to eat and to do, so it was a good fit.

So began our Winter of Shellfish. We had clams in chowder, in clam cakes, on the half shell. We had mussels in white wine, in tomato sauce, in paella. If we were eating something else, like maybe a chicken (hallelujah!), we'd preface the meal with oysters. I rationed out the collards and used the pepper jelly to add both sweetness and heat to stews and stir-fries. We did manage to land a few trout, which I will tell you all about.

I also got lucky because the restaurant down the street had a window box with a robust rosemary plant in it. I snuck down at night with my kitchen shears. That counts, right?

Kevin and I have never before or since eaten so much shellfish, and by April we were pretty desperate to expand our first-hand food horizons. You can imagine how motivated we were to get vegetables in the ground as soon as we possibly could.

PART I

Gardening

CHAPTER 1

WE BEGIN UNSOILED

L et me introduce you to our house.

When we were shopping for it, we told our real estate agent we were looking for a small house on one of Cape Cod's many ponds—a shack on a lake, basically.

Most of the shacks built on Cape Cod waterfront property have been torn down and replaced with much more majestic homes, but ours somehow slipped through the cracks. It was built in the early fifties and measures some 900 square feet. It was very shack-like.

I don't think I realized quite *how* shack-like until our first winter. After the first snowstorm of that first winter, I was at the top of our driveway shoveling the pile of snow the plow had deposited, and met for the first time our neighbor across the street, who was doing the same thing. We introduced ourselves and chatted for a bit, and she mentioned that despite having lived there for fifteen years, she had never seen our house. I of course invited her over, and we walked together down our very long driveway. It took a couple of minutes; you can't see the house until the driveway bends to the left at the bottom of the hill.

She knew it was on the water, and she was clearly expecting the usual majesty. When we rounded the bend, I watched as her face did that cartoon thing when a smile of anticipation morphs into a little grimace of disappointment. Since then, people's reactions to our house have become a running joke between Kevin and me. When they see it for the first time, almost everybody—literally almost everybody—looks around and says, "Nice . . . um . . . nice . . . *spot*," clearly relieved to have settled on the right word.

It is a nice spot. It has privacy and giant rhododendrons and a view of the sunset over the water. The house is much closer to the water than current regulations allow. The lake is clear and cold and deep. So when we first saw the hills and the trees that cover nearly all of the property in dappled shade for most of the summer, we didn't think, *Well, that's not so great for gardening*. We thought, *Nice spot*.

It was only after we'd moved in and started thinking tomatoes that the shortcomings of our property came home to us. And it wasn't just the hills and the trees. It was also the soil; even I could see it didn't look good. In fact, it didn't look much like soil at all. It looked a lot like sand. And the plants that seemed to be thriving were the same ones you see all over Cape Cod: scrub oak, pine, and various kinds of grasses that can scrape by on limited nutrition and prefer fast-draining soil that keeps their roots dry.

The U.S. Department of Agriculture (USDA) confirmed my suspicions, and if you have suspicions about your own soil, they can confirm those, too. They do that with what I think is a remarkable database: the Web Soil Survey. Starting in 1899, the government has been sending soil surveyors out to every corner of our very large country so that we, the gardeners, can know exactly what's in our backyard. Now, 120-odd years in, they've covered nearly 95 percent of U.S. counties, so the chances are good that you can check yours right now. When I first found this out of course I fired up the computer immediately, with feelings of foreboding.

And sure enough, this was my soil profile:

0–7 inches: Carver coarse sand
7–17 inches: Carver coarse sand
17–64 inches: Carver coarse sand

And then it added, "Ha-ha!"

Okay, not that last part, because the government is circumspect about laughing at the agronomical plight of taxpayers. But I can read between the lines.

If you check out the literature on growing vegetables in sand, you will find nothing but pessimism. But I knew that other people on Cape Cod managed to have gardens. Could their soil be that much different? One of the first things we did when we arrived here was join the Cape Cod Organic Gardeners (annual dues: $5), in the hope of tapping into the local expertise. And two of the first people we met were Al and Christl, a couple about our parents' age who have the best garden I've ever seen. On the south-facing side of their house is the spot they call "the riviera," home to tomatoes that produce all summer. Farther down their backyard there are the biggest rhubarb plants east of the Mississippi. And then there's the asparagus.

Al and Christl's asparagus patch has been there for a couple of decades, and it's the purple kind. The first time they gave us some, I was skeptical. The stalks were a good inch in diameter, and I figured they had to be stringy and tough. But seriously, do you really think the best gardeners you know would give you stringy, tough asparagus? It was wonderful and tender and flavorful. And as a bonus, the purple kind doesn't make your pee smell.

Could their success be in their soil?

I hopped back on the Web Soil Survey and typed in their address. I felt like a voyeur doing this, as though if I zoomed in far enough I'd catch them cavorting in the gazebo, so I quickly got the information I needed and zoomed out again.

It turned out that Al and Christl built their garden on something called Hinesburg sandy loam. Loam is, and I'm quoting the Soil Survey here, "a mix of the small particles that form clay, the large particles that form sand, and the medium-size particles that form silt." Okay, that's better than flat-out coarse sand, but nowhere in that description were words like *fruitful* or *fecund*. There were still lots of teeny rocks.

If Al and Christl could grow rhubarb plants the size of a Volkswagen and enough tomatoes to get them through the winter in Hinesburg sandy loam, surely, perhaps with some compost and fertilizer, and maybe a little advice from Al and Christl, we could coax enough vegetables out of Carver coarse sand to keep our first-hand food commitment going.

Just Sow

There's no denying that seeds are miracles. You start with this little tiny roundish thing, add water and sunlight, and get food! At least some of the time.

Seed season takes its time coming to Cape Cod because the water we're surrounded by is quite cold in March and April, and it keeps temperatures depressingly low through what is known as spring in other parts of the northern hemisphere. The joke is that our calendar reads: January, February, March, March, March, June. (The flip side is a spectacular fall; September is the best month to visit, but it's a secret, so don't tell anyone I told you.)

This means that even though you invariably start thinking about gardening in the first March, you can't really do much about it until the third—unless you can give your seeds a head start.

We almost didn't go to the Cape Cod Organic Gardeners' seed-starting workshop. I mean, really, you put the seed in the little pot and give it water and sunlight. It's the stuff of kindergarten projects. But we figured there might be agricultural techniques that weren't covered in kindergarten, so on a brisk second-March Sunday we headed out to Kelly Farm. Its owner, Jean Iverson, who stands a formidable (I am not kidding) four-ten and was then in her eighties, grew way more vegetables than you could imagine a third of an acre could produce. And she could still push the big Gravely rototiller, and no thank you, she didn't need your help.

There were about fifteen of us, and Jean walked us through the process of starting our own seeds. First, you have to use a soil mix specifically designed for the purpose (mostly, that means it has to retain water; seeds don't need fertilizer to germinate since they have their first helping of food built right in). You have to keep them moist but not wet. They have to be in a warm, dark place (indoors) until they sprout, and then moved into the light (outdoors), but still kept warm. We learned to be ruthless in our culling. And we learned about cold frames.

Now, a heat lamp keeps things hot. An icebox keeps things cold. So imagine my surprise on finding out that a cold frame keeps things . . . warm. It's basically a little greenhouse that gives your seedlings, still in their seed-starter soil mix, just enough passive solar to get them through to the third March (that's May, in case you've lost count), when it's probably safe to put them in the ground.

All that was standing between us and our first real vegetable garden was a wooden frame with a glass top, which seemed within our capabilities to build.

By *our* capabilities, I of course mean Kevin's capabilities. When I found him, he already had extensive experience with power tools. I, on the other hand, had gone my entire life up to that point without ever having used one. Building what was essentially a box seemed like it would be a good introduction.

Frame Up

When I lived in San Francisco, back in the eighties, the department of sanitation designated one day a year when they would pick up absolutely anything you left at the curb. I had a group of friends who treated it like a national holiday—Big Trash Day—and we'd go out to see what we could find.

But scavenging seems to be a practice that some people are good at and some people aren't. Although I enjoyed the exercise, I never found anything truly remarkable. My mother, though, knew a woman in New York who found a museum-quality antique bed in the trash. My little brother Jake once found a brand-new wet suit—*in his size*—in a tony part of the West Village.

If you are building a cold frame, I guarantee you could find everything you needed on Big Trash Day. But we don't have that here on Cape Cod. This is unfortunate, in part because we're always doing things like building cold frames.

Luckily, we have the dump.

I know, I know! You're not supposed to call it the dump. It's the "transfer station," an obvious name for the place you go to dump things. And that is what you're supposed to do; there are in fact rules against taking things away from our local transfer station. In general, Kevin and I are law-abiding citizens, but putting things other people are throwing away to good use seems like a pretty good reason to flout the rules.

Besides, if we take stuff away, it really *is* a transfer station. We're just here to lend credibility to the nomenclature.

You do, however, have to avoid the dump workers (*refuseniks*, in family parlance), who sometimes, reluctantly it seems to me, enforce the no-taking-away rule. But discarded windows and doors—which are calling out to be the top of a cold frame—are in the metal pile, and if you back your truck up and create a diversion by discarding some actual metal, you can sometimes sneak out a storm door without calling attention to yourself.

Once you have that, you just need a frame. We planned to make ours out of wood, which meant a trip to the lumberyard. Our first choice of building material was cedar, since it's bug- and rot-resistant. It also ran $5 per board foot, which would have brought our costs for our cold frame up to the $150 range. That was way outside our budget, which was $0 when we began, but which we upped when we realized we'd have to buy framing material. Luckily, treated lumber, which is pine soaked in chemicals to make it bug- and rot-resistant, is much cheaper.

We had heard, as you probably have, that you shouldn't use treated lumber for plant-related enterprises because of those chemicals. So I was delighted to fall back on the one thing that I am actually pretty good at: research. And I am here to tell you that you don't have to worry about it. Back in the day, one of the chemicals used to treat lumber was arsenic, but that was phased out a good ten years ago. The rest of those chemicals might even help ward off pests and fungi (that is, after all, their reason for being there), but not very much because they don't travel far in soil. And no appreciable amount of them will end up in your food.

Treated lumber it was: 1×8s for the sides and 4×4 uprights for the corners. Literally all that had to happen was to screw the 1×8s into the 4×4s, and you're two hinges away from a cold frame.

That, at least, was Kevin's perspective. Mine was that this seemed waaaaay harder than, say, hanging a picture, and maybe we should take a rest and think about it for a while. But it's amazing the difference a little confidence, coupled with an 18-volt cordless DeWalt drill, makes. The ease and speed with which the cold frame came together surprised me. Hanging a picture would have taken me three times as long, with at least twice the angst.

If you're hankering for a cold frame but don't have easy access to cast-off storm doors (or power tools, or Kevin), there is a super-quick and easy option, which I'm sorry to report that we discovered only after we built the storm-door version and figured out we needed an annex to accommodate our rather optimistic spread of seed starts.

This is where I'd try to explain how Kevin's mind works, if I had even the foggiest of clues. But after twenty years with him, I have no idea. No matter what the project is, we tackle it in completely different ways. If there are ten ways to do something, and you ask each of us to list our top five, there will be no overlap.

And so it was, we were in Home Depot, thinking about our need for more cold-frame space. I almost literally saw the lightbulb go on over his head, and he grinned and walked me over to the vents and insulation section. We didn't need vents or insulation, so I had no idea where he was going with this.

He went straight to the window covers—those half domes of heavy plastic that people put over ground-level window wells—and took two off the shelf. Then he took me two aisles over, to the clamp section, and picked up a half-dozen smallish ones. He put the window covers on the floor, back to back, and clamped the seam shut. Voilà! Instant circular cold frame.

I would not have thought of that in a million years, but since he did, you and I don't have to. For under $40, you can build a cold frame in seven seconds. Thank Kevin if you see him.

While I was marveling at my husband's ingenuity, our seeds were busy germinating, and we had our cold frames ready just in time to put our little proto-plants outdoors.

That's when the trouble started.

At least I thought that's when the trouble started. I learned later that the trouble started with the decisions I'd made about the seeds in the first place.

"Oh, no! You can't start delicate plants like cucumbers this early," Christl said when I told her in consternation that every single one of my cucumber seedlings had died just days after we put them in the cold frame. She also explained, as diplomatically as a kind human can, when faced with a friend's boneheaded mistake, that you can't start root vegetables that way at all; those seeds go right in the ground. The fennel plants didn't even have a decent excuse; in the absence of any obvious error, they were irredeemably thin and leggy, the Gisele Bündchens of seedlings. The cold frame was also pervaded by a general air of dispiritedness, which I'm convinced is contagious.

It was a combination of the wrong plants at the wrong time, and I'm pretty sure with just the wrong mojo. A few of our seed starts managed to limp into the garden, but mostly we fell back on the tried-and-true gardening strategy of half-assed gardeners everywhere: we bought a bunch of seedlings, ready to plant. Let's let someone else do this seed-starting job, shall we?

The pickings were slim, but we found a couple of relatively level, sunny spots on our hilly, shaded property to be our actual garden. Then we pulled up all the chickweed, which is about the only thing we can grow in exuberant abundance. (And chickweed isn't like chick lit or chick flicks—there's nothing frothy or ephemeral about it. Chickweed is a formidable adversary.) Once we removed it, we amended our Carver coarse sand with standard-issue all-purpose fertilizer, some amendments a soil test had told us we needed, and what I believe qualifies as a shit ton of compost.

Along the way, we made a mistake that I want to make sure you, the first-time gardener, don't make. Do not, under any circumstances, buy a wheelbarrow.

How could something that's been with us nearly two thousand years and has become a gardening staple, a fixture in every suburban garage, just plain suck?

The wheelbarrow was invented in China sometime in the second or third century AD. I am extremely reluctant to dis anything invented by the same people who brought you gunpowder, the compass, and paper, but the wheelbarrow is just not in that league.

Its fundamental problem is that it has only one wheel. I mean, really, we all know that in order for a structure to be stable, it needs three points on the ground. When the wheelbarrow is idle, it has those three points. But as soon as you pick up the handles, it's got only two: the wheel is one, and you're the other. Oh, sure, you have two feet, but they're not far enough apart to provide stability, even if you're Yosemite Sam. Besides, they're both solidly on the ground only when you're standing still, and most work that involves a wheelbarrow requires going from one place to another.

The point of the one-wheel design, I've been led to believe, is maneuverability. But we all know that *maneuverable* is a euphemism for *capsizable*, which is what the wheelbarrow is. You pick up the handles and start rolling the thing up a rocky slope. You find it requires considerable upper-body strength to keep it more or less level, and you work hard to fight both gravity and instability. Then you trip on a root, and the whole thing goes over.

It's not so difficult if you have a light load, but if you have a light load, you might as well just carry it. The point of a wheelbarrow is to let you transport things that are heavy.

I wasn't willing to launch into a full-scale condemnation of the wheelbarrow until I checked in with Kevin. He often understands the rationale of what seems to me to be a design flaw.

"So what's the advantage of the one wheel?" I asked.

He considered. "You can only get one flat tire," he said. And then added, ". . . at a time."

Well, there's a ringing endorsement.

For subsequent gardens, we acquired a variety of carts, which have four wheels, as well as wheelbarrows that have two wheels in the front, which are fine. I will add, although I understand this is sheer coincidence, that none of our subsequent gardens were the smashing success our first one was.

Harvest Gold!

That first year, almost everything we planted came up roses. Our tomatoes were abundant and sweet. Our kale was sturdy and bright. Eggplants were firm and smooth, cucumbers were crunchy and dense. We had basil, parsley, and chives in abundance.

Sure, there were failures. Our beans didn't like the shady part of the garden we chose for them. Our cabbages were completely devoured by insects. And we won't discuss the watermelon, which was aspirational anyway. But our first-year garden succeeded beyond as wild a dream as I can have about gardening. From about June on, we had no trouble putting something from our garden on every day's menu.

For about seven seconds I was tempted to feel all smug and green-thumby. I fantasized about showing up at the Cape Cod Organic Gardeners' meeting with my cornucopia, crowing about the bounty Kevin and I had wrung from Carver coarse sand. Luckily I thought better of it. It turns out lots of people have good gardens the first time around . . . because the insects haven't yet cottoned on to the presence of a salad bar. But you don't think much about insects in their absence, so after that first blush of smugness, I settled on blind luck as the explanation.

It was probably both, because we never had a garden that good again. But we learned over the years to play to our strengths, to grow what we could grow.

To figure that out, we got help from books and articles and forums and websites, but a funny thing happens when you consult a lot of experts on a topic like gardening: you might come out more confused than when you went in. Sometimes it's because experts will tell you what experts can grow, whereas we needed to know what anyone can grow. Other times, it's because there are lots of subjects that experts disagree about. And still other times, it's because those experts haven't been to your house.

Experts are heavily invested in the idea that experts are required for things. One of my all-time favorite stories along these lines was from *The New York Times*, a couple years back: "Should you take your shoes off at home?" Well, gosh, do we really need guidance on that? The *Times* apparently thought so. "We asked experts," they said.

Plants *are* complicated. Botany is a real subject, the legitimate province of experts. But I found out that you only need to know the tiniest slice of it to grow a tomato.

Gardening is even more local than politics, and the truly helpful experts were our neighbors, fighting the same conditions and soil issues and pests. Christl has taught me more about gardening than anything I've read. But I've learned the most from just getting dirty, from trying things. Some of them worked! Some of them didn't, which is why this book has no chapter on hydroponics, despite the fact that our gravity-fed fertilizer-delivery system was pretty remarkable. Don't try to fight the conditions at your house; if the cilantro always goes to seed immediately, just plant some sage and be done with it. And if you're not sure something's going to work, there really is a best way to find out.

After that first year, the only plants we have grown from seed are the ones that go right in the ground. Sugar snap peas in the spring are always a win. Various lettuces and greens like arugula come up reliably and mature quickly, and we put our cold frames to good use by positioning them over the greens so we could give them a head start. Our collards are usually pretty successful, and we've had years when our cucumbers climb into the trees. Our tomatoes are downright spectacular. Root vegetables, though, we had to give up on. Ditto sweet peppers (although we can do the little hot ones). Herbs, with the exception of cilantro, are a garden mainstay.

Although we don't do seed starts anymore, I don't want to talk you out of them. If you get it right, starting vegetables from seed is incredibly satisfying. Each little paper packet in that big rack at the garden store has the potential to become a bumper crop of butternut squash or Japanese eggplant or pickling cucumbers. Show me another kind of hope that retails for $1.69.

By the time your garden starts to deliver, it won't matter how it began. What matters is the feeling you get when you walk out your door with the kitchen shears to snip off some parsley or a few kale leaves or the eggplant that's going into your dinner. When I started doing it, it was so I could tick the first-hand food box for the day, but the satisfaction wasn't about that. It was some amalgam of accomplishment and sustenance and delicious. That feeling has insinuated itself into my most basic conception of how I eat and how I feed people. I can't imagine giving it up.

I can, on the other hand, imagine doing it with less work. Which is why, at about year six, my head was turned by perennials.

CHAPTER 2

PLANTS EVERLASTING

Tomatoes are like salmon. They're both delicious, and they both put all their energy into reproducing. Then they die.

This is true of most edible things you can grow. Producing cucumbers or eggplants or green beans is a nontrivial accomplishment for plants, and once they manage it, they take their curtain call and go the way of all flesh. If you're trying to grow food year after year, this is irritating. If, like me, you don't find spiritual uplift in the labor involved in gardening, it's downright disheartening.

So if you're like me, you may be attracted by the laborsaving potential of perennials. Just imagine! You plant your garden just once, and then every spring, you sit back and wait for the bounty to come rolling in.

Okay, now imagine a diet consisting entirely of fruit and sunchokes, because that is what you'll be eating. With mint, or maybe chives.

The fruit part is great! Fruits grow on trees and vines and shrubs that are perennial by nature, and they have a vested interest in deliciousness. Animals are supposed to eat them and then poop out the seeds in new territory—the more delicious, the more territory.

Perennial vegetables, though, are nature's cruel joke. She tantalizes you with the idea of automatic food and then delivers almost nothing good to eat.

Sure, for seven minutes every spring, there's asparagus. Alas, asparagus doesn't seem to like the conditions at our house, and we got exactly three spears before our patch gave up the ghost. But if you're interested in the most food for the least work, you should absolutely plant a bed.

There's also rhubarb, which isn't my favorite food, but has earned my affection by being the first plant up in the spring, with foliage that's already luxuriant when other plants are still pressing the snooze button.

And of course we round out the Big Three of Actually Tasty Perennial Vegetables with artichokes. Unfortunately, in another example of nature's sense of humor, the labor artichokes save you by being perennial is more than made up for by the labor they require in preparation.

Yet there are many, many plants that are edible. Surely we can find some decent greens.

Oh, we tried. After five years of garden-variety annuals, with enough experience to know what we could grow and what we probably couldn't, Kevin and I decided we'd restrict our annuals to a few raised beds, where we had the most control over the soil. In the vast, marginally amended expanse of Carver coarse sand that was the rest of our garden, we'd try perennial veg.

But which?

We were looking for some all-purpose greens, the kind of thing you can add to a salad or throw in with a stir-fry.

And now I will invoke the Jake Principle.

It dates back to a time in the mid-nineties when my parents lived in Manhattan, in an apartment with a working fireplace. They didn't have any outdoor space, and my father liked to grill, so they set up a little hibachi in the fireplace. He turned out a mighty nice halibut steak.

My little brother Jake happened to drop in one day when the halibut was on the grill, and it stopped him cold. He looked at the grill. He looked at my parents—prudent, reasonable people. And then he looked at the grill again. "If that was okay to do," he asked, "wouldn't other people do it?"

If your bent is toward experimenting, trying things out for yourself, you will find yourself on this knife edge pretty regularly. Sometimes doing the thing nobody else does makes you a visionary iconoclast, carving a new path for humankind; it is only the danger of asphyxiation from carbon monoxide that prevents the hibachi in the fireplace from falling into that category. Usually, though, it just makes you an idiot who won't learn from other people's mistakes, and that is the Jake Principle. It applies to perennial greens.

I knew the Jake Principle going in. Surely, if perennial greens were delicious, everyone would grow them. But there were just so many candidates, lists and lists! And so many people pushing permaculture, which is the name they've given to agriculture with perennials. We started culling through the lists.

Obviously, you have to eliminate anything these extremely optimistic lists describe as "not for the average palate" or "requires long cooking times." But you also have to cut anything described as "mild," because that means it tastes like grass clippings. From what was left, we zeroed in on two that seemed promising: Turkish rocket and Good King Henry.

The highfalutin names should have clued us in. The guy who decided that *Chilean sea bass* sounded better than *Patagonian toothfish* must have gotten hold of Turkish rocket, because its other name is warty-cabbage.

Good King Henry, like many other borderline-edible greens, is also known as poor man's spinach, and if there's one thing that should make you approach a plant with low expectations, that's it. If it was anywhere close to as good as spinach, it would have its own, more dignified name. *Chard*, for example. Or *escarole*. To be fair, Good King Henry is also known as Lincolnshire spinach, but even though I have never been to Lincolnshire, I'm betting you wouldn't mistake it for Monaco.

To live to see another year, perennial greens have to defend themselves against all comers, and they tend to have robust defense mechanisms consisting of things like hairy leaves and insecticidal compounds. And sure enough, our Turkish rocket and Good King Henry remained insect-free. Our insects, like right-thinking humans everywhere, believed that milquetoast annuals like basil are much tastier than hairy plants with chemical defenses.

We never got past the first tentative nibbles and did not make a single meal out of either Turkish rocket or Good King Henry. But I have to hand it to them—they still come up every year, right next to the chickweed. I don't even remember which is which because I can't be bothered with plants I can't eat.

Speaking of which.

Just about every list of perennial veg includes what were known as Jerusalem artichokes until the Patagonian toothfish guy got hold of them. I'm not at all sure, though, why *sunchoke* is better than *Jerusalem artichoke*. I can understand why you'd want to find an alternative name, seeing as the tuber in question is related neither to Jerusalem nor to artichokes, but that lack of relationship, one would think, would give you an excellent reason to get *choke* out of the name. On the bright side, no poor men are involved.

I was warned about sunchokes. "They'll take over," everyone said, but you already know that I'm likely to see that as a positive. Besides, our Carver coarse sand limits the takeover potential of even the most aggressive plants. We're the only gardeners ever to have a failed crop of horseradish. Still, just to be on the safe side, we planted only two.

They grew, as promised, like weeds. In the fall, I harvested a bumper crop of a vegetable that tastes like a tantalizing mix of Styrofoam and dirt. There is simply nothing to love about a sunchoke. Our pigs wouldn't even eat them, at least right away (leave anything in the pigpen long enough and they'll get around to it).

It is downright ignominious to dig up a plant you put in the ground yourself, but that is what I did.

If you travel in gardening circles, you will find people who are very excited about growing perennials. Their enthusiasm is contagious, and it's hard not to be seduced by the promise of permaculture. But our experience with perennial vegetables turned out to be a waste of time, and even money. I guess that's why they call it *experience*.

Because we've done it, you don't have to. Go with asparagus, undoubtedly king of perennials. Plant rhubarb, which will lift your spirits every April. Devote the rest of your perennial efforts to where the payoff is: fruit.

If you're trying to figure out which fruits you can grow in your neck of the woods, a good clue is what grows wild. Here on Cape Cod, there are raspberries, blackberries, blueberries, beach plums, and grapes.

So we planted a fig tree.

We also planted raspberries, blackberries, blueberries, and beach plums, and made plans for a grape arbor that is, a decade later, still on the drawing board. All our berries—we threw strawberries into the mix—have limped along, and some years we get a respectable haul. It's the fig tree, though, that wheedled its way into my heart.

We knew it was a stretch. It's a brown turkey fig, and I'm still not sure whether it's named that because the fruit bears a resemblance to a brown turkey or because it's a brown version of some other fig that comes from Turkey. If you know, please drop me a line.

Fig trees in general are not cold-tolerant, but this particular variety was specifically developed to have some cold hardiness and was supposed to be able to grow in Zone 7.

If you're a gardener, you already know all about Zone 7, but if you're an aspiring gardener you might not. To help figure out which plants can grow where, the USDA divides the country into plant hardiness zones, based on expected winter low temperatures. If you want to plant, say, a fig tree, you just check which zones it can grow in.

You can't take these classifications to the bank. Although you might live, say, in Zone 7, you might also live, to take an example at random, where it is particularly cold and windy because of proximity to a body of water. If so, your fig tree might perhaps be fooled into thinking you are in Zone 6, where it does not thrive.

We knew that going in and assumed we'd need to wrap it—put heavy mulch over the roots and build a straw-stuffed burlap snowsuit around the tree—to get it through the winter. But we really liked the idea of a fig tree, so we took a flyer.

It started as two sticks, each about three feet tall, with a few buds on it. It was nothing like the fig tree of my imagination, laden with figs the size of golf balls and leaves like the ones in those paintings of Adam and Eve after they decided they needed underpants after all. But we watered it regularly, wrapped it in winter, and for a couple years it grew and thrived.

When it was two years old, we harvested our first figs; I think there were three. But then it had a growth spurt, and in its third year it suddenly started to look like a real tree. It was a good seven feet tall, and it set a crop of so many figs I lost count. There was one in almost every junction where leaf met branch. A hundred and fifty at least.

If there's one thing I've learned about growing food, it's to not count on a harvest until it's actually harvested, and we took no chances. When the figs approached ripeness, we put a net around the tree, anchored to a bamboo scaffold, in an effort to keep birds out. We had learned from our previous experience with netting—when we put a net over a high-bush blueberry only to have a bird get caught underneath with nothing to eat but blueberries—and made sure it went all the way to the ground.

All of you gardeners out there should know that covering fruit with a net freezes it in time. From that day on, the figs stubbornly stayed the same size, the same shape, and the same bright shade of green. I was convinced that up in some attic somewhere was the Fig Tree of Dorian Gray, with soft, brown, fully ripe fruit.

Little did I know, they were just giving the insects time to arrive.

Do you have any idea how many insects there are on this planet? Neither had I, but I looked it up, and it's ten quintillion. That number is necessarily an estimate, an individual census being, up until my figs ripened, cost-prohibitive. But that fall, entomologists had an unprecedented opportunity to do a proper head count, because the moment my figs turned brown, the world's entire insect population assembled in one place.

We had of course encountered insects in our other gardening activities, but nothing that prepared me for that onslaught. In fact, I had harbored the hazy notion that a fig tree on Cape Cod would have relatively few pest problems because the local pests had never seen one. They'd take one look at it, scratch their little insect heads, and move on to something more familiar, like the raspberry bushes, the squash vines, or the delicious wooden portions of our home.

But, in a lesson for toddlers everywhere, you don't get to be ten quintillion strong by being suspicious of a new food. It was also a lesson for gardeners, if not everywhere, at least here in the Northeast: if you hope to harvest a respectable fraction of the food you grow, you probably need to resign yourself to insecticide.

Pests or Pesticides: You Choose

We went into our food-growing venture with eyes wide open. Even though we had a lucky first year, we were under no illusions about pests, and we knew we were willing to battle them with chemicals. We joined the Cape Cod Organic Gardeners not because we wanted to garden organically, but because we wanted to garden prudently and ecologically, and there wasn't a Cape Cod Prudent and Ecological Gardeners to join.

I'm all for pesticide-free gardening. It's friendlier to the planet, it doesn't leave residue on your food, and it's less harmful to the things you're not trying to kill, like ladybugs and frogs. There's only one downside: pests.

I have always suspected that the very idea of organic gardening is a global conspiracy hatched by the pests themselves. They got together to solve the life-threatening problem of pesticides and, in a remarkable show of pan-pest cooperation, launched the organic movement. The leaf rollers wrote the mission statement, the cutworms did the PR, and the slugs—well, the slugs were supposed to set up the website, but they never got around to it.

They left a loophole, though. Pesticides that were "natural" were allowed. "It's natural," they reasoned. "How bad can it be?" You can't fault them for that reasoning, since it's the same reasoning consumers use when paying through the nose for organic produce. Turns out, lots of natural things can kill insects. One of them is a pesticide called spinosad.

The first time some six-legged invader started reducing our collards to lace, somewhere around year two, I wanted to break out the spinosad, but Kevin wanted to knock them back with liquid Sevin, the pesticide of his childhood. He tells stories of picking his father's tomatoes, wiping the white dust off on his pants, and eating the Best Boys and Early Girls still warm from the sun. Since he lived to tell the tale, he reasoned, Sevin can't be so bad.

I am a science journalist experienced at evaluating toxicity evidence, and I could have pointed out that his was something less than ironclad, but nobody likes a pedant.

I did, though, push for my kinder, gentler, less toxic option.

Spinosad has a back story. It's a compound that was first produced by fermenting a soil sample populated by the bacterium *Saccharopolyspora spinosa*. The soil was collected when a vacationing scientist with the natural products division of Eli Lilly stumbled on the remains of a defunct Caribbean rum distillery. He scooped up the sample, brought it back to the lab, and left it to ferment for three years.

What possessed him to let it ferment for three years? Dow Chemical (which now owns that Eli Lilly division) is coy on the question, but I'm betting he just forgot about it. He put the thing in a test tube and then went about his natural products business. Three years later, when he was cleaning out his cubicle, he found it. "Oh yeah!" he said. "Here's that soil sample from the defunct Caribbean rum distillery. I wonder if it's produced any natural insecticides."

Actually, first he probably tested to see if it produced any cancer cures, noncaloric sweeteners, or wrinkle creams. Once he ruled out the big money, he tested for insecticides—and hit the jackpot. Sure enough, *S. spinosa* generated metabolites that were deadly to caterpillars, borers, leaf beetles, and the like, while not harming beneficial bugs like lacewings and ladybugs.

Because it's made by a bacterium found in nature, it's organic. (It's worth noting that this bacterium has never been found in nature again, leaving open the possibility that someone accidentally spilled liquid Sevin on the original soil sample.) Because it's minimally toxic to things other than insects, we gave it a shot.

Turns out it was also minimally toxic to whatever was eating our collard greens. Carbaryl, though, the active ingredient in liquid Sevin, was deadly, and one judicious spraying saved the plants.

It also saved the figs, and my discomfort with industrial-strength pesticides was tempered by my enjoyment of an epic fig crop. But it wasn't just the figs; it was the tree. Anybody who knows anything about gardening would have advised against planting a fig tree in Zone 7 (and some people did), but I have grown to love that tree, struggling to survive just outside its comfort zone, which is obviously Zone 8. And if it takes a little carbaryl every now and then to protect it, I'll do it. Or at least I'll let Kevin do it.

I know gardeners and also full-out farmers who are so skilled that they need very little chemical intervention to grow food successfully. They grow healthy plants, and any healthy plant will stand a better chance than an unhealthy one. Insects, like opportunists everywhere, zero in on the vulnerable—weevil take the hindmost.

Those of us who aren't so great at keeping plants healthy have to find an equilibrium. The planet's tolerance for pesticides isn't infinite, but neither is it zero. We've found, over the years, that spinosad on small seedlings often gives them just enough protection to get through their most vulnerable stage, to a size where they have a better chance. We've also learned that there are some crops where the insects have the upper hand, and we no longer plant cabbages.

Not all pests are insects; birds and mammals can be pestilential in their own right. Our strawberries and raspberries fall victim to chipmunks and every species of bird. One year, in an apparent bid for water in a very dry summer, rats ate almost all our tomatoes. We also have three Asian pear trees, whose fruit we reliably lose to what we suspect is a deer but could be a particularly enterprising raccoon.

Every plant/pest combo forces you to decide just how heroic you want your measures to be. Deer fencing is way too heroic for us and our three pear trees, but it wouldn't be if we had a vineyard. Liquid Sevin may be beyond your particular pale. It's usually beyond mine, but I really love that fig tree.

The winter after our epic fig crop was particularly cold, and the tree died back to its roots. Since then it has staged a partial recovery, but has yet to attain the glory of that harvest. Climate change may be working in its favor, though, and although a flourishing fig tree is small recompense for global devastation, you take what you can get.

Although I'm generally pleased with what we've been able to grow in our distinctly suboptimal soil, I would dearly love an orchard. I want apples, pears, and peaches, pecans and hazelnuts. I want chestnuts. And it's only partly because you don't have to plant them every year. It's mostly because they're trees, which impress not only for their long life and majestic size, but for the sheer volume of food they can produce.

If you're serious about food production, get lots of fruit and nut trees. It'll take a few years for them to pay off, but boy, will they pay off. Kevin and I will come visit in the fall, and lament, again, that we live in a cool, damp, shady place that doesn't lend itself to those crops.

There is, however, a consolation prize for cool, damp, and shady. It took us a few years, but it finally occurred to us that our climate was perfect for mushrooms.

CHAPTER 3

SHIITAKES HAPPEN

Think back for a moment to your seventh-grade biology teacher. Mine was Mrs. Weiss, who told my mother that she thought I was a little too assertive, but also did a memorable experiment demonstrating how we become inured to even very strong smells. And of course she taught us the then-standard-issue taxonomy: kingdom, phylum, class, order, family, genus, species.

There are many mnemonics to help remember this, but all the ones I've encountered have what is a very serious flaw in a mnemonic: they're not memorable. If kings don't actually play chess on fine green sand, how are those letters supposed to help you remember the taxonomy? Besides, there's disagreement about how many categories there are, and which life-forms belong in which categories. Linnaeus, who devised the categories in the first place, can't be expected to adjudicate because he's been dead for 250 years. Luckily, for our purposes here, all that matters is that fungi are different from both plants and animals.

They have their own kingdom because they're weird. The mushroom itself is only the tip of the iceberg. That is, it's the fruiting body of a much larger organism. The bulk of the organism is the mycelium, which consists of long, thin filaments that grow and spread and fuse with other filaments. If you've ever dug a hole and found lots of flimsy white threads, you've encountered mycelium. Although most mushrooms don't even reach the size of respectable grapefruit, the mycelium beneath can reach horror-film proportions, covering tens or even hundreds of acres. (Do you know where your children are?)

The process by which mushrooms reproduce is reasonably well understood. The fruiting body produces spores, which are then carried by wind, water, or any other kind of fungal transportation to a new location, where they try to find other spores in order to mate and create a new mycelium. The conditions in which mushrooms thrive and fruit, though, are mysterious and enigmatic. Fungi in general have proven difficult to domesticate, which is why white truffles can cost $10,000 a pound.

Still, modern mycology has unlocked the secrets of some of the edible mushrooms, which is why white buttons *don't* cost $10,000 a pound; we've figured out how to grow them in captivity, along with a few others, like shiitakes, oysters, and enokis. But for every kind of mushroom grown commercially, there are hundreds known only in the wild, or maybe the basement.

Some of them, of course, we're content to leave there. A lot of mushrooms taste bad, and a few will kill you. But the first guy to crack the code on domesticated chanterelles or morels or black trumpets will make a mint—at least for a while, until everyone else catches on.

You wouldn't think a product that's mysterious and enigmatic would be a good candidate for someone with marginal gardening skills, but it is. Just about every mushroom that can be grown can be grown at home, in ways that have varying degrees of difficulty.

Easiest are the all-in-one mushroom kits where you just add water. If you're a city dweller with no outdoor space, this is the perfect project for you. Although we have outdoor space going begging, I was also tempted by them, but Kevin scoffed. "What's next, a Chia Pet?" He wanted an industrial-strength mushroom project, so we bought ourselves a copy of *The Mushroom Cultivator: A Practical Guide to Growing Mushrooms at Home*, by Paul Stamets and J. S. Chilton.

Let me summarize chapters 1 through 4 for you: Build a sterile laboratory.

Practical, my ass.

Building a sterile laboratory is not the kind of undertaking that plays to my strengths. I've always tended to make hygiene—personal and household—a low priority, and that tendency has been exacerbated by living in the sticks, where I can go days without getting within three feet of another human being other than my husband, whose hygienic standards may be even looser than mine. (Still want to come visit?) A sterile laboratory is a pipe dream when you can't even keep the bathtub clean.

Luckily, that wasn't the only choice. You can also order mushroom spawn from companies that already have sterile laboratories. We've gotten all our mushrooms supplies from an outfit called Fungi Perfecti, but you can also get them from Field & Forest or North Spore.

We zeroed in on shiitakes. Partly it was because they're delicious. But partly it was because they grow in wood. Sawdust works, but so do oak logs. We have many, many oak trees, which are the building blocks of oak logs.

I am, however, wary of any enterprise that starts by cutting down a tree. Part of it is the chainsaw, which always makes me worry about the things *other* than trees with limbs that can be severed. But the other part is that I am fond of our trees, going about their business sequestering carbon, providing shade, and feeding an epic population of winter moths. We have, however, come to realize that the strategic culling of trees—the ones that are sick or threatening to fall on our house or preventing the sun from reaching plants that are supposed to feed us—can work for the greater good.

I think shiitakes qualify as the greater good, don't you?

There was a small oak encroaching on our driveway, making it difficult to maneuver our ever-growing fleet of trucks, boats, and trailers, and we decided it would serve us better as a shiitake farm. We cut it down, we cut it up, and we ordered a batch of small wooden dowels inoculated with shiitake spawn from Fungi Perfecti.

Once you have your logs and spawn, mushrooms are just an afternoon of tedious, repetitive work and then a year's wait away! Spring is the best time to do that work, and the best way to do it is with friends. You're going to have to drill a lot of holes, hammer a dowel into each one, and then cover it with wax.

If you're not sure how to get your friends to do this, reread *The Adventures of Tom Sawyer*, which has a chapter about it. And make sure to promise each of your friends a mushroom log of their very own.

Chances are, either your lack of Sawyeresque persuasive skills or your basic sense of decency will mean that you end up doing a lot of this work yourself. And as your lower back is duking it out with your carpal tunnel to see which can make you say uncle, there will be a moment where you start wondering whether this was really a good idea. But here's the thing about shiitakes: all the work is up front. Once you get this job done, you stack your logs in a shady spot, and you've just set yourself up for many years' worth of mushrooms. The food-to-work ratio here is very high.

After a long afternoon's work, all that's left is the wait.

Like all first-hand food projects, this one comes with no guarantees. Although the dawn of agriculture dates back some ten thousand years, humans have been growing shiitakes since approximately last Thursday. We don't yet know exactly how we can do it best or what can derail our efforts.

If you read the various experts, you'll find that they all say slightly different things—a running theme with experts. If your mushrooms fail to appear, maybe it was because the logs' moisture content was just a little too high or too low. They might be too old. Other fungi may have outcompeted your shiitake spawn. Your spot might be too shady or not shady enough. Too hot, too cold. Venus might not be in the seventh house.

We had at least a few months for all those possibilities, and then some, to cross our minds. Fall was the absolute earliest we could expect a mushroom from our June inoculation.

➤➤ GROWING SHIITAKE MUSHROOMS ◄◄

Timing: Do this in the spring, when your spawn has a chance to start digesting the wood and establishing itself. Use fresh wood, cut either recently or the previous fall, so no other fungi have gotten the opportunity to establish themselves.

Sourcing wood: If you don't have a tree that needs felling or you simply prefer to let someone else handle that part of the job, call your local firewood guy, arborist, or landscaper who helps people deal with trees. There are a lot of them, and you should be able to find what you need, which is hardwood. Oak is reputed to be the best, but people have had success with maple, birch, beech, and hickory. Avoid ash, elm, and fruitwoods.

Log size: The thicker the log, the longer it will keep your mushrooms fed (more wood = more food), and the longer you will get flushes of shiitakes. But thick logs are heavy; don't use anything you have trouble moving. A diameter of 4 to 6 inches works well, and the length can be anything you find convenient. Ours were 3 to 4 feet.

(continued)

Assembly: The objective is to drill a pattern of holes just big enough to accommodate a dowel. Spacing isn't crucial, but holes that are about 4 inches apart, all around the log's surface, will give you enough spawn to colonize the log.

Teamwork: This lends itself to an assembly-line setup. Give one friend the drill, another the dowels and a mallet to hammer each dowel home, and a third some melted wax to smush over each dowel so competing fungi can't take advantage of the breach in the bark. Even though they tell you to use beeswax, nothing bad happens if you use melted votive candles instead.

Stacking: Once the logs are inoculated, find a spot that has some sun and some shade. You can stand them vertically (with one end on the ground) or stack them horizontally, with lots of space in between, keeping them off the ground with a pallet or some kind of structure.

Waiting: Chances are, mushrooms will come in dribs and drabs until the spring after you inoculate. Once your mycelium is well established, a good soaking (by you or a storm) will usually trigger a flush.

Understanding doesn't preclude wonder.

Take airplanes. I *understand* Bernoulli's principle. The wing is curved on the top and flat on the bottom, so the air over the top accelerates and the pressure above the wing drops to less than the pressure below. At speed, you get lift.

Yeah, sure. Next time you fly, take a good hard look at that 757 and ask yourself whether you really believe it can get off the ground. Airplanes are a downright marvel.

Similarly, I understand how mushrooms reproduce. The spores mate and create a fertile mycelium, which feeds off dead or dying wood and eventually produces the fruiting bodies we know as mushrooms. It's as straightforward as Bernoulli's principle. But that didn't stop our first mushroom, which appeared in November, from being a little bit miraculous. There it was, growing right out of the wood. There was only one, and we sautéed it in butter and marveled at the wonder of nature.

By the following summer, we were getting mushrooms regularly. We learned to expect a flush after a storm, since moisture can trigger fruiting. We also learned that, if we needed mushrooms on demand, we could get the same effect by soaking the logs for twenty-four hours. I perfected my mushroom soup recipe (add a little sherry at the end).

Our logs kept giving for about five years; the fat ones went even longer. As I write, we have another batch of logs that should start delivering miracles in a few months.

After a decade trying to grow just about everything, I find shiitakes to be one of my favorites. Give me a box, they check it. They're only an afternoon's worth of work for years of harvest. They're delicious, and the version you grow is often meatier and more flavorful than the version you buy. Their main pest is slugs, which are easily distracted by and then drown in little dishes of beer placed among the logs. When I first did this and counted thirty-seven dead slugs the next morning, I couldn't believe such a simple trick was so effective, but when it comes right down to it, who among us doesn't prefer beer to mushrooms? Even shiitakes.

Our mushroom project was a success on another important front: it pays.

The Garden Math

It sure seems like growing food should save you money, especially if you grow things from seed, but even if you grow things from seedlings. Back-of-the-envelope, the math looks great—even in our most robust year, our seedling budget never hit three figures. How tough can it be to grow a hundred bucks' worth of produce?

But wait! Aren't you forgetting the fertilizer ($65), and the bone and blood meal and various other soil amendments ($47)? There's also the soil test that proved we needed those things ($33). And the seed-starting mix ($18) and the seeds that didn't start ($11)? Oh yeah, the lumber for the cold frame ($19), and the chicken wire for the fencing ($2, at a yard sale)? And you should probably count the little rototiller, even though we bought it used for a mere $25.

Don't get me started on the mileage on the truck and the diesel we burned when we had to go back for one more yard of compost ($30).

We were pretty deep in the red before that first sugar snap pea got ripe in the spring.

But who gardens for the money, anyway? Just asking the question misses the essence of growing things. Gardening isn't about getting vegetables for cheap. You garden to get the backache from constant stooping. You garden to watch the fruit of your labors be destroyed by the vicissitudes of weather. You garden, above all, to ensure that your surroundings have a robust population of well-fed insects.

But there are some plants that pay their way. Shiitakes are one of them. Over the five years our first batch of logs fruited, we harvested at least twenty pounds of them, at $8 a pound. That more than makes up for the $40 the spawn cost.

Herbs also earn their keep, in part because you usually have to buy way more of them than you actually use. A robust parsley patch will keep you in parsley all summer and fall, and those 99-cent bunches you don't have to buy add up.

Garlic and leeks, too. Leeks grow easily from seed, and garlic from garlic cloves, so the effort involved is minuscule. They are virtually guaranteed to reach maturity because only humans like to eat them; neither insects nor varmints will touch them.

And if you can grow tomatoes, you have no excuse not to, even if they don't end up costing less. While not all your homegrown produce will taste better than what you can buy at the farmers market or the grocery store (and I have some green beans to prove it), your tomatoes almost certainly will.

And you don't even need a garden to grow a tomato plant. You can grow it in a pot on the patio or in a basket hanging from the eaves of your house. It's even theoretically possible to grow it indoors, but the lack of pollinators and sunlight are obstacles. And if you're at all tempted to give first-hand food a try, I think you should start with a tomato plant, because tomatoes are surprisingly powerful.

Think about all the people who have tried to convince us to "eat real food." All the people who tell us we're eating crap and it's killing us. And then look at the flat line that is Americans' vegetable consumption. Telling isn't working.

I'm one of the people doing the telling. In my day job, I write about food and agriculture and nutrition for *The Washington Post*. I've written a lot about how the American diet has gotten ever farther from the plants and animals that fueled humans' ascendance to planetary dominance. We now eat things in boxes and bags, labeled with dubious health claims and exciting punctuation. We've lost touch with the plants and the animals, and we have the waistlines and the blood sugar to prove it. But what do we do about it?

Sure, tell people—again!—that eating a whole lot of junky food is bad for you because mortality data. If there's one thing that millennia of human existence and also *Freakonomics* have taught us, it's that we humans don't decide things on facts. A tomato plant has power that peer review doesn't because it doesn't try to persuade you with the correlation between obesity and heart disease. It persuades you with tomatoes.

Modernity has gotten between us and our deep-seated, evolution-endowed sense of what we're supposed to eat, and over the last century or so we've internalized the idea that we need someone else, preferably someone with an advanced degree, to tell us. But, up until about seven nanoseconds ago (evolutionary time), we managed just fine—which is how every other species on the planet manages, too.

A homegrown tomato reminds us, and yes, it shouts, "YOU KNOW HOW TO DO THIS."

PART II

Chickens

CHAPTER 4

COOP DREAMS

Chickens are a first-hand food Rubicon. Gardening, which we were doing with a vengeance, is mainstream, and nobody will look at you twice as long as you're growing standard-issue backyard produce like kale and tomatoes and not, say, sugarcane or sorghum. But as soon as you get chickens, you're serious. Protest all you want about how your house is a Birkenstock-free zone and you don't even *like* crunchy granola. The moment you get your first batch of chicks, you're in the club.

We got ours as soon as they showed up at the feed store.

Our local store, like many others, buys a variety of breeds from the hatchery in the spring and publishes a list of breeds and dates they'll be available. We'd done a fair bit of research on breeds, if you can call poring over Henderson's Handy Dandy Chicken Chart "research." The chart is an online overview of all the major chicken breeds and some of the minor ones, compiled by upstate New York farmer John Henderson. We'd found lots of sources that go into more detail—books, blogs, online forums—but Henderson became our breed bible for its brevity, breed histories, and pithy descriptions (of brahmas: "Some hens ate a lot, got fat, and never laid that many eggs, and we do not currently have any in our flock.")

According to Henderson, Orpingtons are big, cold-tolerant, adaptable to free-ranging, and docile. They sounded like just the thing.

Thanks to Henderson, we also found out they were originally bred in the 1880s in a little Irish town in County Kent called Orpington, by a man named William Cook. Cook's daughter apparently had a hand in the breeding, and together they came up with what has become one of the most popular backyard chickens in the United States.

Imagine living in a town whose claim to fame is a chicken breed. Every time someone asks you where you're from and you say, "Orpington," they say, "Like the chicken?" and you nod wearily and say, "Yes, like the chicken."

The day the Orpingtons (in the most common color, a blondish hue called buff) were due, we planned to get there early. This was 2009, the first year of the recession, and backyard chickens were the new new thing. It wasn't like Black Friday or anything, but there were quite a few people in the chicken line, and we weren't the only ones who were eyeing the Orpingtons. When our turn came, there were only four Orpingtons left. We wanted a full complement of eight and had to round out the flock on the fly. It so happened that they also had Rhode Island reds.

In the course of our chicken "research," we'd learned that the single most important criterion for picking a breed was cold tolerance. Or if you live somewhere warm, warmth tolerance. Your birds have to be appropriate to your climate. Heavy, well-feathered birds thrive in cold places but get way too hot in warm ones. Even if we hadn't, thanks to Henderson, learned that Rhode Island reds were a good pick for us, their New England pedigree was right there in the name. We took four.

It was another lesson in winging it, which became a recurring theme. We'd make careful plans and then end up having to do something else, or maybe something else just started to look like a better idea and we did that instead. And you know what? Nothing bad happens. Okay, *usually* nothing bad happens. There was that one time we planned to make the chicken plucker rotate vertically, but then decided to go horizontal, and the whole thing caught fire, but that was the exception.

In this case, something good happened. Having a mixed flock had two advantages: we got to compare characteristics of two different breeds, and we had at least a fighting chance at telling them apart.

Pre-chicken, it never occurred to us that it would be important to tell the individual birds apart, and that having different breeds makes that a whole lot easier. But it turned out that this was a nontrivial advantage. Chickens are like NASCAR—a lot of the fun comes from knowing who's who. And once you get birds that will thrive in your weather, everything else is just a matter of taste. In later flocks, we risked brahmas, despite Henderson's assessment, because they have feathers on their feet. We got barred rocks because they're attractive and araucanas because they lay green eggs. As long as they're right for your weather, you really can't make a mistake. Go ahead, get the ones with the silly crests.

This is particularly important if you have little kids, who won't be content with a flock of interchangeable birds. They will want to know them as individuals, and they will want to name them. This is an excellent job for little kids, but you have to be prepared to live with the results. My friend Maggie has chickens named Beethoven, Lightning, and Rick.

It took us a while to get to names; we were focused on making sure we saw these teeny-tiny birds through to adulthood. Which meant housing. Which meant a brooder.

If you're picturing the neonatal unit at the hospital, you can relax.

A brooder is just a box. You know how to turn a box into a brooder? Put chicks in it. They'll live there for a month or two, and they need only three things: food, water, and warmth.

The food and water are straightforward. When you buy chicks at the feed store, just look to the right. That's where there's invariably a display of feeders and waterers, which are really just Mason jars with plastic lids that look like cartoon UFOs. You put the food or the water in the jar, turn it upside down, and the food or the water comes out into the UFO.

I worried about the warmth part, but it turns out you don't have to. Read about raising chicks, and you learn that they need a temperature of about 95 degrees in their first week, and you have to reduce the temperature by 5 degrees every week until they're happy at room temperature. This sounds awfully specific, but think about it for a second.

Out in the real world, you know who raises chicks? Hens. That's right. Birds with single-digit IQs and no thermometers. If the chicks are cold, they snuggle under the hen. If they're hot, they venture out. And they do the same thing with the heat lamp you clip to the side of the brooder. If they're too cold, they huddle under it and you know you have to move it closer. If they're too hot, they avoid it and you know you have to move it farther away.

Our brooder was a plastic storage box. We cut out half the lid and replaced it with wire mesh (we wanted it to be secure because there was a cat in the equation). We lined the bottom with paper towels. The chicks were fine with it.

The difference in the breeds was apparent from the get-go. The reds zoomed around with confidence and aplomb while the buffs went about their business quietly and, apparently, contentedly.

This has happened to me a lot, and I'm betting it's happened to you. You watch a kid experience something new—food, toy, weather, animal—and you get this mishmash of feelings about how great it is that kids take joy in those things, and nostalgia for your own childhood, and regret that you don't get that feeling much anymore. One of the best things about venturing into chickens is that you get that feeling.

Here's something that humans have been doing for millennia and that people all over the world take for granted, and you—adult you—get to try it for the very first time. Even now, with a mere decade of experience under my belt, I've drifted away from the "exciting new thing" category, and when I see new chicken-keepers obsessively posting pictures of their growing chicks, I nod and smile and find myself feeling a tiny bit smug. Yeah, been there, done that, and done that, and done that again.

But the smugness is wrong, partly because smugness is pretty much always wrong but mostly because that was me, ten years ago. I blogged about our food adventures regularly, and I subjected my readers to the selfsame indulgent, obsessive posting of pictures of our growing chicks.

And you know what? It was fun. We'd never hung out with baby chickens before, and they were cute and, in a limited kind of way, fascinating. We put a little roost bar an inch or two off the ground so they could jump on it. If an ant wandered by (we live in the woods and this does happen), we fed it to them.

The cat, though, was more fascinated than we were. She seemed inordinately excited by the prospect of having very small birds in the house. Kevin liked to let her commune with the chicks—through the cat-proof brooder—on the theory that we could teach her that the brood is a part of our family community and therefore not acceptable prey. I, however, had very little faith in our cat's community spirit and preferred to keep a closed door between them. (The balance of power in that relationship shifted as the chickens grew, and as soon as they seemed more threatening than delicious, the cat ignored them in that way cats do.)

They grew so fast that they were discernibly different, if not every day, certainly every other. Within a week, they went from being fuzzballs with round heads and toothpick legs to proto-chickens, with necks and thighs, distinctly less cute. We watched as their wings got longer, their legs got sturdier, and their fuzz gave way to feathers.

Three weeks in, they started spending all their time on their phones and pretended they didn't know us. Chicken adolescence comes at you fast, and the birds got mangy-looking, with clumps of chick fuzz on their as-yet-unfeathered necks and heads. Their first awkward attempts at flight had them falling all over one another. I don't think you can watch another species grow from infancy to adulthood without getting a sense that we're all related.

Size-wise, they got too big for the brooder but were still too small for the coop, so we had to rig up tweener housing for them. Since they were going to be in it for only a month, we didn't want to call in the Toll Brothers, so we went scavenging to see whether we couldn't house them with repurposed materials. We salvaged a crate from the dumpster at the local equipment rental place, wrapped it in some chicken wire from behind the garage, and the chicks liked it fine. (Pro tip: If you're building animal housing, the dumpster at an equipment rental place is a great place to start.)

We put them in the garage, where we could shut them in at night for safety but open the doors during the day for sunshine. It wasn't pretty, but it was serviceable housing that would last them until they came into their majority and moved to the coop. Which, while all this was going on, we'd been building.

Or more accurately, Kevin had been building, and I'd been trying to let him do it unmolested.

Kevin and I live happily together. I put this down to the fact that we agree that a spouse should be trustworthy, considerate, and entertaining, and we both exert ourselves to be that kind of spouse. We do, however, have one deep-seated difference, not so much of opinion, but of temperament: Kevin solves problems once and for all, while I'm makeshift through and through.

Take the leaky refrigerator we had in New York. As soon as we discovered the problem, Kevin began looking into bigger, better refrigerators, while I just put a bowl on the top shelf to catch the drips. The leak got worse, and Kevin suggested that since we were replacing the refrigerator, perhaps we should remodel the kitchen. I got a bigger bowl.

The bigger the project, the more apparent the difference becomes, and the chicken coop was our first major construction project. Not skyscraper major, but definitely backyard major, and our temperamental difference was an issue from the beginning.

I believe this difference has a strong genetic component. In part, this is because I believe most things have a strong genetic component, but it is also because my mother, in this regard, is just like me. Possibly worse. Take, for example, the mailbox incident.

I grew up in Poughkeepsie, New York, a town about 80 miles north of New York City, on the Hudson. We lived in an ordinary suburban neighborhood, in a very unattractive raised ranch with four bedrooms and a two-car garage, on a quarter acre with a lawn, driveway, and mailbox.

We were the neighborhood weirdos, a designation I thought a little unfair given that the neighbors right down the street from us let their grass grow waist-high and kept their umpteen children locked indoors. But I guess their isolation kept them under the radar, and it was our family that was the target of occasional neighborhood vandalism.

When the top of our mailbox loosened enough so it could be detached from its post, our rather unimaginative neighborhood vandals started to make a habit of detaching it and depositing it somewhere nearby, where we would eventually find and recover it. When the post came loose from its concrete mooring, and you could lift the whole assembly right out of its hole, someone did. After we found the mailbox in a neighbor's yard and brought it home, my mother decided she'd had enough. She didn't put it back in its hole. She put it in the garage.

If Kevin had lived with us then, he would undoubtedly have gotten a new mailbox, poured a solid concrete anchorage, and installed it in such a way that, come Armageddon, it would be the last mailbox standing.

My mother put the mailbox out every morning and took it in with the mail.

This wasn't a terrible system, except for the mornings when we didn't get the mailbox out in time. On those days, we would hear the mailman coming, dash down to the garage, and then run out to the end of the driveway carrying the mailbox. There were mornings when we didn't even have to put the thing in its hole—we just held it out to the mailman and then brought it back to the garage with the mail inside.

My affinity for such solutions—let's call it the mailbox gene— governed my idea of what a chicken coop should be. Kevin had plans for a coop for all time, a veritable chicken Parthenon, encased in a covered run furnished with all conceivable chicken luxuries. I kept thinking about that refrigerator box in the garage.

When my mailbox gene crosses Kevin's Parthenon gene, we often finesse the issue by invoking one of the bedrock principles of a successful marriage: non-overlapping magisteria.

The term was coined by the late evolutionary biologist Stephen Jay Gould, in an essay about reconciling science and religion. In it, he made the case that they didn't need to be reconciled, because each covers territory outside the domain of the other—i.e., non-overlapping magisteria. *Magisterium* is most often used to mean the teaching authority of the church (from the Latin *magister*, or teacher, as Google informed me), but it can also mean the office of a person in charge of something, and that is the sense in which I use it.

Every marriage has its magisteria, and it's better for all parties if some of them are non-overlapping. If, for example, one spouse—let's go out on a limb and say it's a woman—stays home, keeps house, and raises children while the other goes to work and makes money, you have large, well-defined non-overlapping magisteria.

Most modern marriages have less clearly defined magisteria. Kevin and I both work, and we work together to keep our household running. Even so, it shakes out so that some jobs are exclusively mine, to do as I see fit, while others are his. I do the laundry. He string-trims the grass. I am Vice President of Cat Puke Stain Removal, while Kevin is Director of Chainsaw Acquisition. Our different temperaments make themselves known in these jobs. Our clothes are indifferently laundered, but we have a top-of-the-line Husqvarna.

Non-overlapping magisteria do an end run around potential causes of friction, but they are sometimes hard to maintain because they require one party or the other to butt out.

Butting out is not my long suit. Which brings us back to the chicken coop.

I knew that Kevin's philosophy, born of his Parthenon gene, was the better way to go for our chicken coop. Chickens have to be protected from predators. They need a house that will last at least as long as they will. You can't do it with chewing gum and sealing wax. Besides, Kevin had much more experience building things, and it made a great deal of sense to let this be his job.

That is what I was determined to do, knowing that in the long run, I would be very happy with the result. But my mailbox gene would not be quelled. I couldn't help myself. I trespassed on his magisterium. Maybe it could be six feet tall instead of eight? I suggested. Or maybe we could use fiberglass as the roof of the run? Wouldn't three nest boxes be plenty?

I'd like to think I did it because I believed that the potential improvement my ideas could bring outweighed the disadvantage of violating the boundary of his domain—after all, there are situations where the thoughtful input of both of us yields better results than either of us could achieve independently. The reality, though, is that I did it because butting out is not my long suit.

Kevin, to his infinite credit, didn't say, "Butt out of my magisterium," but instead gave my suggestions due consideration—he even adopted one or two. If this was Kevin's subtle strategy for getting my buy-in for the Parthenon, it was genius; there's nothing like having skin in the game to commit you to a project.

The process of designing and building the coop—it ended up being 87 percent Kevin, 6 percent Tamar, 7 percent accident—taught us a lot. First, it was another lesson in the importance of firsts. You learn way more the first time you try something than in any other iteration. Sure, if we built a second one, we could make it a bit better, but it would never top the increment of going from knowing nothing to having built a chicken coop.

One of the other important lessons, which Kevin figured out early on, is that you don't really build a coop for chickens. They'd happily live in your car and lay eggs in your hat. You build a coop for you. You're the one who'll have to refill the feeder, change the water, harvest the eggs, and clean out the coop, and your design should make those things easy. The chickens' needs are small: they like stuff on the ground to scratch in, roost bars to roost on, nest boxes to lay eggs in, food, and water.

Both you and they would prefer that predators be kept out, and that's the top priority for coop design. In our neck of the woods, we have raccoons, coyotes, opossums, fishers, hawks, and foxes, and every single one of them wants in.

We made our chickens' new home from rough-sawn 1×10 pine from our local sawmill. The coop itself—the box they go into at night, with roost bars and nest boxes—is 8 feet long, 4 feet wide, and about 4 feet high, with four nest boxes and several roosts made out of tree branches. It's got a sloping roof covered in Tyvek and roof shingles, with a ridge vent on the high side. It has a window.

The coop is attached to the back wall of the run, which is 8 by 16. Its base is bordered with 6×6 treated lumber, with wire mesh underneath it, so that anything that tries to dig under will hit wire rather than chicken.

Our plan was to build a coop you didn't have to clean out. Poop is probably the biggest downside to livestock, and the less you have to deal with it, the more likely it is that you will continue to keep livestock. Chicken poop is an excellent kind of poop in that it breaks down very quickly. We covered the base of the coop in a thick layer of pine shavings and the floor of the run with dirt and wood chips. The poop composts directly into whatever you've put on the coop floor (you might have to add more of it every now and then) and basically disappears. Once a year, we shovel out the coop, use the compost on our garden, and put in a fresh layer of pine shavings.

The key to not having to clean the coop is deep litter, and keeping chickens this way is called, sensibly, the deep-litter method. We wouldn't have it any other way.

The only other consideration was proximity to electricity, and this is where I have to introduce you to Aunt Dag.

My great-great-aunt Dagmar Dahlquist had been brought up to work in her parents' central Minnesota grocery stores, and that was what she did. In 1925 she was forty-three, and everyone assumed that she would live out her life a spinster, behind the counter in the grocery in Carlos.

Then one morning a recently widowed farmer named Frank Palmer came into the store. Dag had known him for years; he came in regularly and was a fixture in the community. On this particular morning, he had clearly dressed carefully and seemed intent on a purpose.

"What can I do for you, Mr. Palmer?" Dag asked him.

"You can marry me, Miss Dahlquist."

She did. And she entered into a life that required a slate of skills she didn't have. She didn't know the first thing about chickens, horses, cows, sheep, or pigs, all of which were resident on the Palmer farm. She'd never had so much as an herb garden. She couldn't even cook. (She *could* fix a truck, but Frank didn't have one.)

She took this in stride and did what any red-blooded self-respecting middle-aged woman would do. She learned. She learned from Uncle Frank; my mother, who spent summers on their farm in the 1940s, learned from both of them.

When I told my mother I was trying to figure out whether we needed electricity in the chicken coop, she didn't laugh, but she said Uncle Frank would have. "They didn't even have electricity in the farmhouse, and if people could get by without it, chickens certainly could."

In a rural community in the 1940s, people took chickens in stride. Everyone had them, nobody made a fuss about them, and even the little kids knew how to take care of them. Since then, we've lost the connection to the idea that chickens are just part of life, and now building a coop and getting a flock seems like a big hairy deal. If we'd grown up with Uncle Frank, we all would have known how to raise chickens by the time we were six.

In the modern world, most of us don't have Uncle Frank. But Uncle Frank didn't have YouTube, so maybe we're even. There are so many resources out there that all you have to do is type "Do I need electricity in my chicken coop?" in the search bar, and a picture of Uncle Frank, laughing, will come right up. But scroll down and you'll find actual answers.

No, the coop doesn't need light or heat or phone chargers. But if you live in a place with subfreezing winters, your choice is to constantly lug unfrozen water out to the coop (and if you're considering this, I suggest watching the Gérard Depardieu movie *Jean de Florette* before you decide) or to put in a heated platform, available at any feed store, that you can put the waterer on. I recommend the heater. And I'm betting that Uncle Frank, if he'd had both YouTube and electricity, would have agreed.

⟫⟫⟫ CHICKEN BASICS ⟪⟪⟪

If you're going to cross the chicken Rubicon, here are the most important things to keep in mind.

1. **Check the rules and regs.** Lots of cities, towns, and homeowner associations restrict chickens; many have a maximum number, prohibit roosters, or have an out-and-out ban. And even if you're within your rights, best to talk with your neighbors. Chickens can be loud, but enough eggs to share can make it all worth it.

2. **Choose the right breed.** The most important consideration is that the birds are appropriate for your weather. Big, feathery breeds thrive in the cold but wither in the heat. Little froufrou chickens are better for warm climates. Second most important is broodiness, the mode hens switch to when it's time to raise chicks. A broody hen undergoes hormonal changes that have her sitting in the nest box, guarding the eggs with her life. She leaves the box just long enough to get food and water to sustain herself, which is critical if you're planning on raising chicks, but undesirable if you're not. If chicks are in your future, you need a motherly breed like a buff Orpington. If not, stick with the birds that don't go broody, like your all-purpose, no-nonsense Rhode Island red. The single best overview of chicken breeds ever assembled is Henderson's Handy Dandy Chicken Chart. Definitely google it.

3. **Know your predators.** Chickens taste like, well, you know, and every predator in your neck of the woods will be after yours. The

(continued)

nocturnal ones, like raccoons and coyotes, are comparatively easy to protect against; you just have to make your coop predator-proof. But if you plan to let your birds roam free, daytime predators like hawks and foxes can make it a dangerous proposition. Know your landscape and prepare accordingly.

4. **Build Fort Knox.** No matter what kinds of predators you have, they will try to get into your coop, which has to be sturdy and well protected. Walls made of chicken wire (or some other kind of wire mesh with small holes) spanning columns is fine for all but the strongest and most determined carnivore, but don't forget about the floor. Span the base of the coop with wire mesh so anything trying to dig under hits mesh rather than chicken.

5. **Don't crowd them.** One of the primary determinants of whether there's peace in the coop is space. If they have enough and don't feel like they're competing for food, you're much less likely to get into a warlike situation. The rule of thumb is 2 to 3 square feet per bird in the coop, 8 to 10 feet in an outdoor run, but I'd go with at least 50 percent more. And include at least one nest box for every four or five birds. Advice on this is all over the map, which means the number of nest boxes isn't critical.

6. **Build the coop for your convenience.** It's there to protect them and to make caring for them easy. Are you putting it near an outlet so you can use a water heater in the winter? Are the nest boxes accessible from outside? Is it tall enough so you don't bump your head every single goddamn time you go in? Is it easy to refill the feeder and waterer? Build it for you. They'll be fine.

7. **Don't clean the coop.** Okay, it's not don't clean the coop ever. It's don't clean the coop more than about once a year. When you use the deep-litter method, where you cover the floor with a few inches of whatever—straw, wood shavings, leaves—and periodically add more, the poop composts, and there's very little smell. Once a year or so, harvest the fertilizer.

8. **Have an exit strategy.** If you're in it for the eggs, it's best to keep birds for about two years and then replace them, because their production drops dramatically as they get older. If you're not inclined to eat them yourself, find someone who is. If you want them to live out their lives in comfort, prepare to have pets that will live several years past their egg-laying prime.

9. **Forge ahead with confidence.** Humans have been keeping chickens for millennia, since way before the internet was there to answer your questions. It's not difficult. Once you have your coop built, it's also not time-consuming or expensive. And eggs make the best hostess gift ever.

This book and this list are not going to answer all your questions. This is all intended to be a jumping-off place, to arm you with basic know-how and baseline confidence. For the rest, there are books, the nice people at the local feed store, those backyard chicken forums, blog articles galore, and innumerable other resources. If you don't know, ask. If the answer is straightforward, you'll find it right away. If people disagree, it probably doesn't matter very much.

Go forth and chicken-keep.

If I Had to Hammer

I helped with some of the coop construction, but that help consisted mostly of holding things in place while Kevin secured them with power tools. When I took my turn with the framing gun, we discovered what became a recurring theme in our projects. On the one hand, each of us wanted to develop new skills, but on the other, we wanted to get the damn job done. The best way to get the damn job done is to let the person who's better at a particular task just do it. This is known as the Competent Spouse Doctrine.

According to it, when we're framing things, Kevin should use the framing gun, because he can zap in three nails to my one. But since Kevin's better with *every* tool (and most construction-related jobs), where does that leave me?

On the coop roof, with a hammer.

We'd picked up some cheap remaindered asphalt roof shingles, and the very last step in coop construction was nailing them in place. After watching Kevin do a couple rows while I did absolutely nothing, I couldn't take the efficiency one more minute.

"Let me do some of that," I told him.

He stopped hammering. He blinked. He climbed down and handed me the hammer.

The last time I'd spent any quality time with a hammer, it was probably the Fisher-Price kind that blooped when I was trying like hell to get the square peg into the round hole. But I certainly understood how hammers were supposed to work, so I climbed up, put a nail in place on a shingle, and missed the thing altogether.

Once bitten, twice shy, and the next few strokes hit the nail, but with all the force of a butterfly's kiss.

"It's all hand-eye coordination," Kevin said. "It's like a golf swing. You have to trust it."

I know from experience that people are sometimes surprised that people who build chicken coops, scrounge in dumpsters, and practice questionable personal hygiene also play golf, but there you have it. I started playing in earnest when we lived in New York, and it taught me something I'd previously had very little opportunity to learn: to trust my body.

We used to play a lot with our friend Ann, a natural athlete who routinely trounced me by ten strokes. I told her, on more than one occasion, that it was frustrating to try and improve at something when you have no talent.

"How do you know?" she asked.

How did I know I've got no athletic ability? I couldn't quite get my head around the question.

"Yeah, how do you know?"

"Well, I was always picked last in gym class unless Caroline Miller was in it."

"Do you have any more recent data points?" One of the reasons Ann and I are friends is that we are both hard-assed empiricists.

Golf taught me that my body has the almost miraculous ability to swing a club over my head and bring it back to a little ball enough of the time that I mostly score in the 90s (although I am capable of some spectacular streaks of incompetence). It taught me that I can't micro-manage the club back to the ball; every golf swing is an act of faith where you trust the connection between your eye and your hand.

Hammering was just like that. You take the hammer back and trust that your brain will guide it back to where you want it. I focused hard on the head of the nail, took the hammer back, and brought it down, hard.

On my left thumb. It hurt like hell.

The next time, though, I actually hit the nail.

After I'd been hammering for a while, doing my best to trust my hand and eye, it started taking me fewer strokes to get each nail flush, and more of them were going in straight. I still couldn't get a nail in with two strokes, the way Kevin could, but I was neither embarrassing nor injuring myself.

And this, I am here to tell you, is the secret to successful self-improvement: getting a little better at things you're already good at is WAY harder than getting a lot better at things you're terrible at. I can toil over the keyboard for the rest of my life and never write like Anthony Trollope, but in a single afternoon I can learn to use a hammer.

I finished the roof and climbed down to admire my work. It was only then that I noticed that the part Kevin did was nice and flat, the way a roof was supposed to be, and the part that I did had two big lumps running through it.

"You didn't stagger the shingles," Kevin told me, "and the lumps are where they overlap."

Here's where Kevin's excellence, both as a partner and as a human, was on full display. He had worked on this coop for weeks, first designing it and then building it, and I swanned in on the very last day to make sure there were two giant lumps on the roof. But all that mattered to him was that I was happy to have learned how to hammer. He didn't give a damn about the lumps.

And, lumpy though it was, Kevin's coop scored a coup of *Architectural Digest* proportions when it was featured on the home improvement website BobVila.com, which noted its efficient layout and overall attractiveness. Our coop was—and is—secure, spacious, and convenient.

It was also expensive.

How expensive? I'm glad you asked, because I added it up:

Treated lumber and wire for base	$196
Pine from the sawmill (first trip)	231
Pine from the sawmill (second trip)	110
Pine from the sawmill (third trip)	32
Miscellaneous hardware and parts	144
Roof shingles	53
Feeder and waterer	45
Chicken wire for run enclosure	40
Run door and decorative rooster	15

That comes to $866, and it's not even everything. I didn't count hardware we already had, the used table saw we bought to rip 1×2s, or the new blade for the used table saw. I also didn't include the bale of bandaging material we went through when Kevin nailed his index finger to his middle finger with a Porter Cable FR350 framing gun (speed comes with risk). Or the framing gun. But even if you just factor in the brooder and the chicks themselves, we're definitely into four figures.

We didn't go the first-hand food route to save money, although it sure would be nice if we could, and this was some serious cash outlay. I'd hoped that these chickens would (eventually) pay for themselves, and since we were out of pocket at least $1,000 before we had egg number one, I was at first pretty skeptical.

Now, many years later, from the vantage point of having done just about every food project known to man (and run the numbers on all of them), I'm happy to report that the chickens are one of the winners—if you're in it for the long haul.

A hen in her prime will lay a dozen eggs in about two weeks. In that time, the food she eats (three-ish pounds) costs less than a dollar, and even less than that if you supplement with kitchen scraps or free-range foraging. Given that fancy-pants eggs easily cost $4 the dozen, and sometimes twice that, it's a win even when you factor in the overhead of chicks and chick feed, and amortize the coop.

But there's a catch. The math works only if you actually eat the eggs.

Kevin and I eat eggs, but not every day and not in huge quantities. We've had chickens for more than a decade, and we've given away literally hundreds of dozens of eggs. That doesn't save you money, but it sure does make you friends. It's also fodder for the vibrant bartering that goes on in every community where people grow food; we've traded eggs for jam, pickles, asparagus, venison, and tomato seedlings.

Eggs, though, aren't the only benefit to keeping chickens. Another is chickens.

CHAPTER 5

CHICKEN OUT

When we first got chickens, almost all our predators were nocturnal. Raccoons, opossums, and coyotes all live in our neighborhood, but they generally come out at night, which makes it reasonably safe for the chickens to range free during the day. We didn't have, for example, foxes (cue the ominous music), so we could let them wander in relative safety. Our one daytime predator, the red-tailed hawk, was a danger to smaller birds, but wasn't really a match for a large hen. So we gave them the run of the place.

We loved having chickens roaming the property. They're not as good company as dogs or even cats, but they'd always mosey on over when we were working outside, and what certainly seemed to be curiosity endeared them to us. And inevitably it endeared some more than others.

I won't declare unequivocally that all chickens have personalities. We've certainly had some who never distinguished themselves in any way. But we've also had a couple who were downright charismatic.

Blondie was the first. She earned her name in the same way our cat, whose name was Cat, earned hers. Maybe Kevin and I need to consult some little kids, because we are pathetically unimaginative namers of things—someday I'll tell you the story of how we named the boat—and the chickens who had names (not all of them did) had pathetically obvious ones. Blondie was blond. Buff, actually, as in buff Orpington. She seemed like she was a shade lighter than the others, so there you go.

Now that I've actually used the word *charismatic*, I have a hard time justifying it. Blondie's claim to charisma was that she seemed to want to hang around us, and she liked to peck at our shoelaces. It didn't surprise me at all that this was sufficient to earn my affection, but it surprised me quite a bit that this was enough to earn Kevin's.

Kevin really took to the chickens. He would pick them up and stroke their feathers and cluck "Who's your daddy?" at them. He would feed them good things to eat. He would involve them in his projects.

I was touched by this because Kevin is super tough. He embodies a panoply of old-fashioned virtues. Honor. Courage. Perseverance. Grace in the face of adversity. Although these are fine qualities in anybody, it seems to me they make a man manly. Kevin is strong and daring and fearless. He's not fazed by hard work or getting dirty. And he never complains. If something hurts, I don't hear about it until it's time to go to the emergency room. He barely flinched when he nailed his two fingers together.

He loved communing with the chickens. He watched how they interacted, and he understood their individual whims. When one of them got separated from the others, he helped her find the flock.

One afternoon I was working in the house when Kevin walked in after being out in the yard for several hours. I had a question for him—I have no idea what it was—and I started to ask it when he interrupted me mid-sentence.

"Hold on," he said. "I promised the girls some corn." He got a scoop of corn out of the fifty-pound bag on the porch and scattered it outside for them.

"Did you just interrupt me so you could give the chickens corn right this very instant?" I asked when he came back in.

"Well," he said, obviously not having seen it in this light, "I did promise."

He loved all the chickens, but he definitely loved Blondie best. One day we had friends over for lunch when she wandered over to check out our shoelaces. Kevin picked her up and tucked her under his arm.

He introduced her to Rick and Mary Ann. "This is Blondie."

Rick and Mary Ann said hello.

"She likes a little chest massage," he explained to Rick as he rubbed the base of Blondie's neck. "Who's your daddy?" he said into her ear.

And then she shat on him. All over his shirt and shorts.

You'd have thought we were in junior high, given how funny we found this. And Mary Ann told me the next day that Rick reenacted the scene several times that night, with their cat, Gracie, playing Blondie. "Who's your daddy?" he'd say. "Do you like a little chest massage?" And then he'd make a farting noise and two intelligent, sophisticated adults would collapse in laughter all over again.

This is what chickens bring to the party. But who among us couldn't use a little comic relief?

In the first few years we lived on the Cape, there were a couple of stretches that were particularly stressful for Kevin. He had been a commodity trader, working on the floor of the New York Board of Trade, when we lived in New York, but the internet changed everything. Commodity trading underwent a wholesale transformation, with open outcry—the ring of people yelling and gesturing at one another on the exchange floor—being phased out in favor of online trading. The skills weren't wholly transferable, and Kevin was trying to figure out if he should still be a trader or direct his attentions elsewhere. He'd been a trader his entire adult life; it was integral to his identity. Not doing it felt like cutting off a limb.

When it got bad, I'd sometimes find him hanging around outside with the chickens, just watching them. If they were in the run, he'd take a chair in there and just sit with them. For a while it was about the only time I saw him relaxed and happy.

"Hell will freeze over before I'm jealous of a chicken," I told him during one of those stretches, "but I hope the time will come when you can again find happiness in other things as well."

That time did come, but the chickens that helped my husband through a particularly tough time earned my affection for every member of their species.

Nice chicken story, yes? And it's just the kind of story that helps the birds preserve their wholesome image. What's more charming than hens roaming around your property, enhancing your well-being while providing natural insect control? And this does happen. But I feel duty-bound to tell you about the downside, too.

Chickens are actually vicious little dinosaurs. If you have chickens and you have a garden, the chickens will expend all their time and energy, as well as whatever intellectual horsepower they can coax from their seven brain cells, trying to get into the garden.

And no, they're not going to eat the weeds and the bugs and leave strategically deposited fertilizer. They're going to eat the tomato that's one day short of perfect. When that's been pecked to a seedy red pulp, they'll start on the tomato that's two days short of perfect. Only after they've done irreparable damage to all the things you want to eat will they move on to the things you don't want to eat, like the bugs and the weeds.

The last straw was the window boxes. We thought they were safe, because although chickens technically have the ability to fly, they're nobody's eagle. We discovered, though, that they will push their substandard capacity to its limits for access to herb-filled window boxes. (If your chickens are like my chickens, they won't care for tarragon or chives, and these will become mainstays of your recipe repertoire.)

We tried signage: No CHICKENS! But you can guess how far that went, and we ended up just shooing them out of the window box and threatening them with dire consequences if they came back.

"Watch it," I told them. "There's more than one way to be stuffed with herbs."

We had no choice. Fences it would have to be.

Good fences may make good neighbors, but they make disgruntled chickens. At first the hens treated the fence as a curiosity, something interesting that happened to have sprung up between them and the salad bar. But I had built it, so of course it consisted of a few sticks and a roll of chicken wire, patched together with some sealing wax and chewing gum. They just squeezed under it. Only when I put down a few strategically placed rocks did they seem to grasp the significance of the two-foot-tall expanse of chicken wire.

We got to an imperfect but acceptable equilibrium. The chickens got to run around, and they only occasionally broke through to indulge their hankering for our produce. It worked just well enough that Kevin didn't feel the need to step in and build a real fence.

Since it was important to me to have happy chickens, I couldn't help but wonder whether getting fenced out of the garden took a toll on their well-being. But how do you figure that out? How can you know if a chicken is happy? Hell, I can't even understand *people's* happiness unless it's derived exactly the way mine is. If it makes you happy to fish, to camp, and to binge-watch *The Good Life* (do it if you haven't yet), I get it. But if opera, kayaking, and adventure travel float your boat, your psyche is a mystery to me.

While I have an abstract understanding that different people enjoy different pursuits, it still boggles my mind that something that bores me witless can fascinate someone else. Someone of the same species, someone whose DNA is virtually indistinguishable from mine. How can it be that a person who is the product of the self-same set of evolutionary forces actually enjoys nonrepresentational art?

And if I can't begin to get inside the mind of a fellow human, what hope is there that I can understand an animal? Oh, sure, there's less to understand, but there's much less common ground from which to understand it. Remember those Fancy Feast commercials? The one where the cat food went on a little crystal pedestal, and the announcer went on and on about all the ingredients that might sound appetizing to humans? I always thought they were silly because everyone knows a cat would rather eat mutilated chipmunk guts out of a hole in the ground.

What, then, do chickens want?

I do know that our free-roaming chickens absolutely, positively preferred to be out of the run than inside it. They told us so, loudly, every morning. When we opened the run door, they ran outside and did the chicken dance. If for some reason we had to leave them inside, they'd stomp their little chicken feet and get their little chicken picket signs and stage a protest. "Free range! Free range!" was their rallying cry.

But what if they don't know what outside is like? Fast-forward a few years, to the end of our chickens' free-ranging lifestyle (cue the ominous music again). Chickens that had never been outside, or who hadn't been outside for quite a while, didn't protest. They seemed perfectly content to stay in the run. The only thing they seemed to get excited about was snacks, which we brought them regularly.

Our locked-in chickens never know inchworms or basil or fence-breaching, but we have seen no signs of discontent. Although I can't see into their little chicken brains, I know they don't fight, they don't bully (much), they don't get sick, and they don't try to escape. They have food, water, lots of space, protection from predators, comfortable nest boxes, and plenty of roosts. If you provide those, your chickens will probably be fine. As my husband is fond of saying, "It's all about the *husband*ry."

Which Came Second?

When our first flock was about five months old, we got our very first egg.

Our first egg ever. We wanted to preserve the shell, so we did the pinprick trick and blew out the contents. Kevin scrambled it; two bites each.

I still have the shell, and I still remember that it was way more exciting than it had any right to be. It's an EGG. Hens have been laying them, and people have been eating them, for thousands of years. But this was a reprise of the feeling of getting our first chicks, and of so many other firsts: the thrill of discovery compounded by the brain-stem-level satisfaction of raising food.

Thousands of eggs later, the feeling is less acute, but it's never gone away. Walking out to the coop in the morning, opening the nest box door, and collecting breakfast feels so solid, so constructive, so connected—and I also get to check off my first-hand food of the day before I've even finished my coffee.

I know those eggs come from hens with good lives, and eating them feels different from eating other eggs. And that feeling gives rise to a very common misconception: that backyard eggs taste better.

I am here to tell you that they do not. I can hear you spluttering! I have never gotten as many angry comments and letters as I did when I wrote about this. My piece was in *The Washington Post*, but it got picked up in quite a few other news outlets (so controversial!), giving lots of people the opportunity to get mad at me.

I understand. I do. When I went into this, I assumed that backyard eggs from overindulged chickens would taste better than lowest-common-denominator supermarket eggs. But after eating them for a while, I wasn't at all sure. They pretty much tasted like eggs.

There was only one thing for it. We hosted a blind egg tasting. We invited six of our closest friends, several of whom are food professionals, and fed them soft-boiled samples of our eggs, regular supermarket eggs, supermarket organic eggs, and fancy-pants Country Hen organic eggs.

It was not a dignified event, because the key to a blind egg tasting is actual, literal blindfolds. Eggs from backyard hens and those from hens fed certain kinds of feed will often be a different color; they'll be less pale, maybe more orangey. And if they're fresher, as eggs you just gathered from your backyard are going to be, they're going to stand up higher and have whites that adhere better because they haven't lost the carbon dioxide that will slowly seep through the shell.

If eggs look different, it's very easy for them to *seem* to taste different, so blindfolds it was.

If you're wearing a blindfold, you of course can't feed yourself, so you have to sit there and be spoon-fed, dignity be damned. At least two shirtfronts never recovered.

The upshot? No one could tell the difference. The tasters' comments were all over the map—each kind of egg got both good and bad assessments—and the best-in-show vote was split almost evenly among all four. Mostly, we determined, eggs taste eggy.

When I wrote the story for the *Post*, I checked in with a bona fide poultry scientist to see if my results jibed with the understanding in the industry. Oh, yes, they did. She told me that when they did blind tastings (which they do by manipulating the lighting, thus sparing their tasters the blindfold and the mess), they got the same result: nobody could tell the difference. For unblinded tests, though, people had very strong opinions. Yes, the egg with the brighter yolk tastes better. And the brown egg tastes better than the white (or vice versa, depending on which kind you ate as a kid).

In fact, every truly blind egg tasting I've ever heard of has come to the same conclusions. All eggs taste the same. Yet nearly everyone who raises backyard chickens or eats eggs from the ones their neighbors raise is persuaded otherwise.

It goes back to that feeling I get when I pad out to the chicken coop in my bathrobe and slippers to collect my breakfast. The idea of backyard free-range eggs is so much more palatable than the idea of hens kept in small cages for their entire lives (the norm for the industry, though it's beginning to change) that it's natural to think that the eggs themselves must also be more palatable.

What, then, is the point of disabusing people of that idea? Aren't I just denying them that pleasure, to no real purpose?

There is a real purpose. Many of us who believe livestock should have a decent life are trying to convince American consumers that it's worth it to spend a little more for eggs, milk, and meat from well-treated animals. One of the arguments, often, is that those products taste better.

If those products don't taste better, the American consumer who ponies up the extra bucks only to find that the expensive stuff tastes just like the cheap stuff is going to feel, quite rightly, that she's been sold a bill of goods. It'll make it very easy for her to tell herself that people advocating sustainable, animal-friendly farms are blowing smoke.

If those of us who care about these things are going to convince people to buy products from farmers and growers who look out for the well-being of their livestock, we have to push the products on their genuine merits. If free-range farmyard eggs don't taste better, it doesn't do those of us who oppose keeping animals in cages any good to go around saying they do. What's important about eggs has little to do with the eggs themselves and everything to do with the chickens who lay them. So let's just say that.

Garbage into Food

When we first got our birds, most of what I used to put in the compost—apple cores, cucumber peels, collard stems—went to them instead. It took some time for me to fully understand the wide range of garbage that can be turned into eggs by a flock of chickens.

For starters, there's what's left when you make stock. I never throw away a bone or a meat scrap, and I make stock whenever Kevin starts looking askance at the bone bag in the freezer. I use the pressure cooker, and what's left is a pile of soft bones and scraps. Once the stock solidifies in the fridge, there's also the fat on the surface. The chickens get both, even though that makes them cannibals. Happy cannibals. They love the stuff.

Then there's pie crust. I knew they like grain, and I knew they like fat, so the little scraps that are left over after I shape a crust should go over well, I reasoned, as they are made almost exclusively of grain and fat. *Well* is an understatement.

If they like pie crust, perhaps they like all baked goods. If I let a slice or two of bread get moldy, the shame is somewhat mitigated by the enthusiasm with which the chickens devour them. When circumstances landed us with a box of apple cake mix that I was not inclined to turn into apple cake, Kevin stirred the raw mix together with some stock fat, and the chickens went wild.

But they don't go wild for everything. My chickens' markedly different reactions to different kinds of foods—which are a lot like mine—are a lesson in evolutionary fitness. Okay, I don't want the raw apple cake mix tossed with chicken fat. But I'd go for an apple cake, and the chicken fat is lovely when it's enriching a soup.

The chickens love any kind of protein food—the stock leftovers and fish skins—and grains and fats are also high on their list. Like humans, they seem to prefer calorie-dense foods. Vegetables, they can take or leave, just as so many of us humans can. And they can convey their preferences just as clearly as the toddler who throws the broccoli at you. When I walk into the coop with a bowl of something, the chickens mill around eagerly. When I toss it on the ground, either they start pecking like mad or they take one look at it and then look back up at me. "What else you got?"

It's the cooped-up version of what they do when they roam free. Top of their priority list is insects, which they are very good at spotting. And then they go after plants they consider tasty, which are unfortunately the same ones you consider tasty. When they've exhausted those, they'll pick at the grass. And so, in the coop, they leave the parsley stems and cauliflower leaves and carrot tops for last. They do eventually eat them, but I think it's because they're bored and it's variety.

I like it that the chickens eat the garbage. I love the barnyard alchemy that turns scraps and grass and insects into eggs or pork or milk. When the feed is something humans raise for the purpose, like hay or grain, it's not so magical. After all, if we're raising crops, we might as well raise something we can eat ourselves and skip the middleman. But if the feed is a by-product, or something humans can't (or won't) eat, or just plain trash, it's like getting something for nothing, like spinning straw into gold.

"The chickens are like Rumpelstiltskin," I told Kevin as we watched them eat some corn that had begun to ferment in the refrigerator. "Garbage goes in, eggs come out."

"How do you know?" he asked.

What do you mean, how do I know?

"I mean, have you ever actually seen a chicken lay an egg?

At that point, I hadn't.

"Maybe the chickens aren't Rumpelstiltskin at all. Maybe they're the girl, and Rumpelstiltskin sneaks in at night?"

Oh, please. Chickens lay eggs.

"Think about it," he said. "We're the king because we lock them in the coop, and if they don't lay eggs, we kill them, right?"

Well . . . yes. "Who's the girl's father, the miller?"

"All those people who tell you that chickens lay eggs."

This is what chickens have done to the level of discourse in our house.

The End

"If you've got livestock, you've got deadstock," my friend Jen told me. Jen is a New Englander, but she moved to the UK when she married a man whose profession doesn't even exist in the United States. Mike is a gamekeeper. His job is to manage the pheasant population on an estate on the Welsh border so that hunters will pay good money to pursue them with guns.

Managing a pheasant population also means managing the fox population, and Jen once shot one out her window, in her underwear. She's the only person I know who's done that.

Jen also trains gun dogs, maintains their kitchen garden, and raises sheep. She is a woman of skills, with much experience of animal life and also death.

If you're getting chickens and you take a moment to think about it, you undoubtedly hope that they die before you do. But when it happens, that doesn't make it easier. Especially when a predator is involved.

When we let our first chickens run free, we knew we weren't making the safest choice. We could, theoretically, have guaranteed their safety by keeping them locked in the run. The decision we faced—liberty or security?—is the decision all animal owners face, because animals want to do dangerous stuff.

Cats want to prowl the woods at night. Dogs want to stick their heads waaaaaay out the window. Pigs want to break out of their pens and explore a major street (ask me how I know). And chickens? Chickens sure seem to like being out in the fresh air and sunshine, scratching and pecking and dust-bathing.

The problem is that fresh air and sunshine is where the predators are, so it's risky. And it gets even riskier when the trees lose their leaves, giving airborne predators an excellent view (this mattered more when bald eagles moved into the neighborhood). In the winter, we always kept the chickens cooped up, since the lack of foliage, combined with the lack of insects and greenery to eat, changed the risk/reward calculation.

Occasionally, though, we made an exception. And so it was on one December day about three years into our chicken adventure, when it was sunny and almost 50 degrees. I had to go into the chickens' run to put the water heater in for the winter, and going in and out is easier if you're not trying to keep the flock from making a break for it every time you open the door. So I let them out. They did the "yay, we're outside!" two-step and then scattered to see what kind of meager offerings they might be able to scratch up.

About an hour later our next-door neighbor David came over. "I've got some bad news," he said. "There's a very dead chicken in our yard."

It was Phyllis, a small, bright white araucana.

She was one of our favorites. From the very beginning, she distinguished herself. She wasn't warm and fuzzy, like the buff Orpingtons, or sensible and approachable, like the Rhode Island reds, but she was ballsy and curious. She'd come right up to you, but she wouldn't stand for being picked up. She had her own agenda, Phyllis did.

She got her name because Kevin and I had an argument about her. He thought she was a pullet surprise (you have to say it out loud to get the joke), which is when a rooster sneaks into your batch of hens—it happens, because the sexing process isn't perfect. He figured any bird that was ballsy and curious must be a rooster. I reminded him that ballsiness and curiosity were by no means the exclusive domain of males, and that she was just a ballsy, curious hen (I was right). When I posted a picture of her on the blog, an astute commenter noticed an uncanny resemblance to Phyllis Diller.

Phyllis wasn't the first bird we'd lost to a hawk; the runt of that group of chicks got picked off when we set them up in a little day camp the previous year. But she was the first adult, the first one we'd had a chance to know personally. And she was dead because I'd let her out.

It's not easy, finding the right balance between an animal's liberty and its security. We have coyotes here, but we always let our cat go outside because that's what she loved to do. As it happened, she lived seventeen years and died of kidney failure, but it might very well have gone differently.

Neither fences nor judgment can be perfect. You do your level best. Knowing that you've done your level best is cold comfort, though, when your imperfect judgment costs an animal its life.

That day put an end to winter holidays for the flock, but we continued to let them out in the warmer months. As bad as I felt about Phyllis, I knew that losing just one bird in three years of chickens meant that it was reasonably safe. So from May to October, we freed them in the morning and closed the door behind them when they came in at sunset.

Until the day I came home to a scattering of brown feathers in the driveway and a disquieting silence. I went looking for the flock, and found another scattering, this one of white feathers. I found the white chicken, dead and still warm, in the woods. No other birds were in evidence.

I walked the property and finally heard a rustle in the leaves. I thought it was the chickens, but it wasn't. It was a fox, skulking around behind the garage.

Kevin and I stood vigil until sundown, when two of our ten birds came tentatively out of their hiding places. We ushered them into the coop, locked them up, and got up at dawn the next day to see if there were any more stragglers. One more appeared midmorning. Several days later, I got a message from a neighbor, who'd woken to a chicken eating the spillover from her bird feeder and thought it might be one of ours. It was, and we brought her home.

One of the four we recovered died a couple days later, either from injuries or from PTSD, and that left us three. Three, where ten had been. It was gut-wrenching.

Foxes are daytime predators, and from that day to this, the chickens have lived in the run. We miss having them as part of our landscape, and their company when we're working outside, but it's the only responsible choice.

There's a strong case that death, not eggs, is the best reason to have chickens. A visceral connection to the animals that supply our tables was a matter of course for most people, throughout most of human history. Internalizing the idea that death has to happen in order for us to eat meat or cheese or eggs makes you think differently about meat and cheese and eggs. I never eat any of those things without considering their animal of origin.

Teaching us to rethink our food is a tall order for a laying hen, so it'll come as a relief to her that the process really doesn't have much to do with thinking. It's more like those frogs in the boiling water. Those poor guys get asked to carry an awful lot of metaphorical weight, but that's what happened to us—us Americans, not us Kevin and Tamar—and our food choices. It's not like one day you just wake up and decide that today seems like a good day to switch from oatmeal to Froot Loops. You get inured to a society where Froot Loops are the norm, so that's what you eat. Normal moved ever farther away from actual plants and animals, and we just got used to it.

Chickens are an antidote. They're a daily reminder that food has to come from somewhere. But be warned: they could be the beginning of the end. Chickens are a gateway livestock, and as soon as you get used to having them and their steady supply of eggs, you're going to start thinking about what other animals you could add to the barnyard. Is goat yogurt calling to you? Interested in raising your own Thanksgiving dinner? First-hand food is vulnerable to mission creep.

A backyard coop is the perfect challenge. It's hard enough to push you a little, but not so hard that you'll just press the snooze button and stay in bed. I came out of it with some basic construction skills, a much better sense of how Kevin and I work best together, and a never-ending supply of eggs.

The best thing about it, though, was that I went from never having built anything to having built this one thing, and it's that jump from zero that puts you on the steepest part of the learning curve. That's where you're most likely to find that sense of childlike wonder that most of us haven't felt since we were actual children.

Hell, if you can build a chicken coop, what can't you build?

PART III

Fishing

CHAPTER 6

FEAR OF FALLING (IN)

First-hand food is an exercise in opportunism. There's only so much your climate, your soil, and your topography are willing to give, and that's where you focus your energy. I am envious of those of you in Southern California who can grow avocados and tangerines. Also you guys on farms in the Midwest who have access to corn-fed venison. And anyone in morel territory.

Here on Cape Cod, though, we have fish. World-class fish.

Kevin grew up on Long Island, fishing, and he was ready to get a line wet the moment we landed here. I grew up landlocked, not fishing, and was less eager.

"Not fishing" isn't technically true. My connection to Cape Cod started when I was a kid, when I spent summer vacations on a lake called Peters Pond. Although I went there literally every one of my first sixteen years, I went fishing exactly once. It was with a friend and her dad. The dad caught a trout. My friend and I caught nothing. It took a long time. It was hot.

Fishing, I concluded, sucks.

That is where my mind was when Kevin announced he wanted to buy a boat. Because at that point we really had no idea where our next dollar was coming from—and also because I thought fishing sucked—I was not enthusiastic. Although I definitely wanted to add fish to our food-a-day rotation, I thought we might be able to do that without venturing far enough from shore to require a boat.

Over that first winter, in a pleasant break from clams, we did.

Our house is on a lake very much like the lake of my childhood. It's about 110 acres, 60 feet deep at the deepest point, and stocked with trout. My understanding is that the conditions are hospitable to trout survival, but not trout breeding, so there isn't a self-sustaining population. There are, however, lots of small- to medium-size young trout and few large, wily old trout. And as soon as the pond iced over, about midway through our first winter, people came out to catch them.

Usually the danger of winter activities comes from speed. Skis and snowboards and luges are perfectly safe as long as you're not moving. Although ice fishing has the virtue of not involving speed, it more than makes up for that by happening on ice, through which you can fall to your death. I'm not normally a cringing, sniveling coward, but there's something about the idea of falling through ice into freezing cold water that scares the bejeezus out of me. Which is why, initially, I wasn't ready to ice-fish until I saw with my own eyes something very heavy—a Bradley Fighting Vehicle, or maybe a rhinoceros—safely traverse the ice on our pond.

Kevin, on the other hand, was suiting up as soon as the ripples stopped. And so, one sunny January day, he talked me into taking a walk on the ice around the edge of the pond. When we started out, the ice did indeed seem reassuringly, even rhinoceros level, solid.

Halfway round, we ran into two ice fishermen. They had several holes going, were burning wood in a grill to stay warm, and were, inexplicably, drinking beer. After we chatted with them for a while about technique, we went on our way.

"How can they be drinking beer when it's twenty degrees out?" I asked Kevin.

"You're supposed to drink beer when you ice-fish," he explained. "That's part of the point."

We worked our way around the pond to the public beach at the south end, where we met a father and son who had apparently come there with the sole purpose of walking out on the ice. They went out what seemed perilously far, but they looked unconcerned. I was beginning to get the sense that I was the only person on the Cape afraid of the ice.

But when we reached the north side, we felt a little shift. The movement was accompanied by the weird noise ice-covered water makes. It's an eerie, echoing twang, as though Zeus is flexing his cookie sheets or Shamu is very sick. If you are inclined to be afraid of the ice, it's not helpful.

"That's completely normal," Kevin reassured me. As I mentioned before, I am not a cringing, sniveling coward, and also the water under us by the shoreline was probably knee-deep at most. By the time we finished our circuit, I was ready to acknowledge that the ice was clearly safe some distance out, and I was determined to give this a shot.

We had the ice and the will, but we didn't have the gear.

And here I will invoke one of the first principles of fishing, which is really one of the first principles of living.

We all have basic principles that help us navigate the world. You already know about the Competent Spouse Doctrine and the principle of non-overlapping magisteria, both of which help us with division of labor. Others help us deal with some of the less consequential aspects of life. One of my favorites, borrowed from my friend Rafe, is "Never refuse a mint." Miss Piggy contributes "Never eat anything you can't lift." The only billionaire of my acquaintance adds: "Always do a billionaire a favor."

"Make friends with fishermen" is just the fishing formulation of what is perhaps the most basic rule: Be nice to people. I think it's important in every endeavor, but in first-hand food, where useful information is more likely gleaned from locals with experience than from books, it pays particular dividends. Not that we're in it for the dividends! At least not most of the time. Niceness greases the skids of civilization and makes all interactions go more pleasantly for all concerned. I am a big fan of niceness.

But it can play out in your favor at the bait and tackle shop, which is where you will undoubtedly find yourself if you're learning to fish. In our town, the bait shop is Sports Port in Hyannis, and its owner is Amy.

Amy is undoubtedly aware that people come in to try and wheedle information out of her, and I have to believe that she thought I was being friendly and engaging because I was trying to charm her out of everything she knows. Which, in a way, of course I was. Luckily, Amy also believes in niceness, and we had a nice long talk about ice fishing.

She explained that in winter, the fish hang out near the bottom, so you want your bait to hang out there, too, and she showed us how to rig a tip-up so the shiner (the little fish you use to catch the bigger fish) stays where the trout are likely to be. The tip-up is a gizmo that you lay across the hole you made in the ice, with a reel extending below and a flag on a spring above. It's rigged so that, when the fish takes the bait, the flag springs up. We bought three.

Before you set it, you obviously have to make a hole in the ice. I had imagined this was a delicate operation, performed with a precision tool designed to drill a hole with minimal disruption to the surrounding ice. The ice you're standing on, that would be. There is such a tool. It's called an auger. But we didn't have one, so we had to go to plan B, which involved an eight-pound maul. A maul is like the infertile offspring of a sledgehammer and an axe. It is not delicate or precise. It is designed to beat your chores into submission.

"Don't worry," said Kevin. "Everyone uses these."

"Not those guys," I said, with some trepidation, pointing across the ice at two people who were using what I strongly suspected was an auger.

Kevin waved his hand in dismissal and made a noise like *pffffft*.

Kevin, as you may have gathered by now, is something of a risk-taker. I have resigned myself to his participation in dangerous activities, but I haven't quite gotten to the point where I participate with him. Mauling the ice seemed to me to qualify as a dangerous activity, and even Kevin admitted it had a certain counterintuitive element. But we tied a long rope to a tree, so we'd have something to pull on if we fell through, and we got on with it.

We went out about fifty feet, and Kevin started whacking away at the ice with the maul. Chips flew in all directions, and in moments we had a trout-sized hole. Nothing had happened, and we had all three tip-ups set in short order.

The existence of tip-ups makes all the difference in ice fishing. It means that, instead of sitting next to the hole jiggling a line up and down, you can set it and retreat to more hospitable accommodations to watch for a flag. In the case of the neighboring ice fishermen (and they were all men, although I reserve the right to use *fishermen* as a gender-neutral term for all people who fish), that meant hanging out around the Smokey Joe. In our case, to the sneering disapproval of ice fishermen everywhere, it meant sitting in our living room.

At last! I get to retreat to the familiar territory that is my armchair.

Because hanging out on the ice in relative discomfort is supposed to be part of the experience (or so Kevin says), you could say that retiring to comfortable chairs next to a roaring woodstove is unsportsmanlike.

Although if you have the opportunity to do it, you're much more likely to say could you hand me my slippers.

It's almost embarrassing to tell you how exciting it was when that first flag went up. We saw it release, and we both pointed and yelled. "The flag's up, the flag's up!" It was kind of like a fire drill—we grabbed our boots and hats, and we ran for the exit. We went down to the ice and raced out to the hole. Somehow I wasn't scared anymore.

We reeled in our line and found nothing. No trout, no bait. The fish had grabbed the shiner and made a break for it. We reset it and went back in the house.

After another half an hour of not catching anything and using the binoculars to watch other ice fishermen not catch anything, we got another flag. Same drill, same drama, but this time: a beautiful 2-pound rainbow trout.

It is stupidly, wildly, unexpectedly exciting to catch a fish. It is absolutely the difference between not liking to fish and liking to fish. I can't even tell you how we cooked it, but I can tell you what a wonder I thought it was—dinner, caught by us, right in our backyard.

We ice-fished all winter, and the only mishap didn't involve the ice at all. It was when I had the brilliant idea of using goldfish from the pet store instead of shiners from the bait store, on the theory that they were brightly colored and would attract more trout, and also that they were cheaper. It was only after the first two escaped that I realized I was releasing carp, a notorious invasive species, into our pond. This is incredibly stupid, as well as being illegal.

"If this was okay to do," I heard my little brother Jake ask, "wouldn't other people do it?"

Luckily, I can report that there have been no carp sightings in the pond for a decade, so I will not go down in history with the zebra mussel guy and the kudzu lady. But what this incident shows, other than the aforementioned incredible stupidity, is that I was thinking about fishing.

When spring rolled around, and Kevin started talking about buying a boat again, I was ready. I *wanted* to fish. Although there are fish you can catch from shore, you have to wait for those fish to come to you. If you have a boat, you can go to them.

Our Ship Comes In

Anyone who has either owned a boat or watched *Jaws* understands how important size is. The thing you're buying is going to venture out onto actual water, which is voluminous, powerful, and indifferent to your survival. Unfortunately, though, you shop for boats mostly on land, where even small boats tend to look large.

Kevin and I took a hard look at our fishing needs, our finances, and our towing vehicle, which at the time was a 1970 Land Rover series IIA, and decided we should be looking in the 15- to 17-foot category, with me leaning toward 15 and Kevin leaning toward 19.

Fifteen feet was big enough to navigate the bays and harbors we were planning to fish, Cotuit and West Bay on the south side and Barnstable Harbor on the north. In appropriate weather, we could venture farther out, to Nantucket Sound on the south side or Cape Cod Bay on the north. Fifteen feet is also easily trailerable and small enough to be powered by a motor with horsepower in double digits, considerations for, respectively, mobility and economy. Because we wanted a boat primarily for fishing, and not for drug-running or party giving, a boat that size seemed about right to me.

Then Kevin found a 19-foot Eastern, a very basic open boat with a center console, powered by a 70-horsepower Johnson outboard, on Craigslist. When we went to look at it, I balked. On its trailer in the parking lot, it looked like the *Queen Mary*, but Kevin obviously wanted it.

Although I wouldn't go so far as to call it a rule, Kevin and I do have a guideline about resolving situations where we don't agree: let the person who cares more make the decision. In this case, not only did Kevin care more, he *knew* more—which meant he'd be doing the lion's share of the work involved in maintaining the thing. So of course we bought it.

We took it for its inaugural voyage on a warm, breezy July afternoon. There's a network of three bays on the south side of Cape Cod, and the ramp to the northernmost is just a couple miles from our house. We dropped the boat in without incident, but as it was sliding off the trailer into the water, I was troubled by something that I thought wasn't supposed to happen in boats: water was accumulating in the stern.

By the time Kevin parked the truck and we backed away from the dock, most of the water was gone, which struck me as rather mysterious until Kevin explained scuppers to me.

If you look it up, you'll find that a scupper is defined as "an opening in the side of a ship at deck level to allow water to run off."

It was undoubtedly my ignorance showing, but to me this sounded an awful lot like a hole, something I thought boats weren't supposed to have. Absent some fancy valve mechanism, I would think that the same "opening" that lets water out would also let water in.

Which it does, of course. What turns a hole into a scupper is its position. Below the waterline, it's a hole, and water comes in. That's what happened when we angled the boat into the water from the trailer. But when the boat levels, the scuppers go back above the waterline, where they belong. Which is where they stayed as we tootled south toward Nantucket Sound, with Kevin at the helm and me lolling in the bow, thinking how very spacious the boat was.

The bays are protected, so the breeze didn't raise much in the way of a wave. The engine seemed to work as well as a ten-year-old engine could be expected to, and we cruised south without incident.

There's a barrier island, Sampsons Island, between the bays and Nantucket Sound, and a narrow inlet on each end. Kevin took us out the west end and into the sound. All of a sudden, the terrain shifted. The waves were feet instead of inches, and as the boat rode up them and plunged down them, I felt my heart beat faster. I knew that, as waves go, these were pretty tame. I knew that the boat was built to handle much, much more serious water than this.

But it's a visceral reaction.

I wouldn't quite call it fear, partly because I knew we were well within the boat's capabilities and partly because calling it fear makes me look like that sniveling coward I keep insisting I'm not. But it was definitely . . . anxiety. I was not, at that point, used to being on the water, and the bang of a hull as it comes down on the far side of a wave was outside my ken.

Over the sound of the engine and the slap of the boat against the water, I heard Kevin saying something to me. I couldn't quite make it out, so I turned around to face him and put my hand to my ear. He repeated it, and this time I heard him quite distinctly.

"You still want a smaller boat?" He was laughing. Laughing!

No. No, I didn't want a smaller boat, thank you very much.

CHAPTER 7

ONE FISH, TWO FISH, START WITH BLUEFISH

Kevin grew up catching bluefish, and he assured me that if you're going to learn to fish, you couldn't ask for a better beginning. They'll sink their teeth into anything they catch sight of, moving or still, living or dead. They eat fish, shellfish, eels, and squid . . . but also each other, and jewelry. They prefer their prey to be smaller than they are, but bigger isn't a deal-breaker; they've been known to attack humans. They eat when they're not even hungry (although I'm not sure how researchers figured that out), and they kill just for the hell of it.

One of our first trips out for bluefish took us through that same cut Kevin had used to persuade me that bigger boats were better, and we hadn't gone half a mile into the sound before we saw a splashing scrum of jumping fish.

I was amazed at the melee. An area of water as big as our house was roiling with fish. They were leaping and squirming, seemingly oblivious to the presence of our boat.

Kevin handed me a rod, rigged with a metal lure. "Cast right into them. You'll get one every cast."

Every cast? Surely not.

Every cast. My lure hadn't been in the water three seconds before I had a fish. I was using a light rod with six-pound test, gear typically used for small fish, and it bent double. The bluefish wasn't big, but it fought like it was. The fish was taking out as much line as I was reeling in, and it wasn't until I tightened the drag and gave the fish a little time to get tired that I made any progress landing it.

Land it I did. After that, we landed nine more, our limit. There were also the three that got away, and the one that fell through the hole in the net, deliberately bitten by his predecessor in a final act of rebellion. All of this took about fifteen minutes.

There's fishing, and then there's catching. Catching definitely does not suck.

From that day to this, bluefish fishing has been my favorite kind. Pound for pound, they put up a very good fight. They're easy to find, and they're often around in quantity; once you figure out where they are (they're not usually making a ruckus on the surface), you can keep trolling over the same spot and get a fish nearly every time. If you have friends who think fishing is boring and you want to prove them wrong, this is the way to do it. You'll come home with a full cooler.

The problem, of course, is that the cooler is full of bluefish. You've probably heard some variation of the joke about how to prepare this fish. Fillet it, brine it, and cook it on a plank over a low fire for an hour—then throw away the fish and eat the plank.

A lot of the people who hate bluefish have just never had a properly handled, truly fresh specimen. It degrades very quickly, so if the fish isn't put on ice promptly and turned into dinner within a day or so, you might very well prefer the plank. If, however, I serve you a blackened bluefish sandwich made from a fish we just caught, you will never again laugh at that stupid joke.

The sandwich is a bluefish fillet, coated with a Cajun-style spice mix (we make our own, heavy on the smoked paprika, but you can buy one ready-made), blackened in a hot cast-iron pan, and served on robust bread with caramelized onions and tartar sauce. You can also put fresh bluefish right on the grill, or bake it with mayonnaise, mustard, and herbs, but the sandwich is our favorite après-fishing meal. It has converted many a bluefish skeptic.

All the bluefish that don't get eaten in that first meal go into a brine and get smoked the next day. With its strong flavor and high fat content, it smokes beautifully, and smoked is the hands-down most popular way people eat bluefish in these parts.

Having voiced my full-throated, deeply felt defense of bluefish, I will acknowledge that there are fish in these waters that I prefer.

⋙ HOW TO SMOKE A BLUEFISH ⋘

The success of your smoked bluefish starts when you bring it into the boat, which is when you do three things:

Bleed it. The hemoglobin in blood accelerates oxidation (which leads to rancidity) when it's exposed to air, so having less of it in the fish is a good thing. You do this by cutting the gills, either with a knife or scissors. Make one cut on either side, hold the fish head down, and it'll bleed out.

Wait for it. Oxidation happens when fish is exposed to—you guessed it!—oxygen, one of the main ingredients in air. And, in a rotten-fish twofer, air also converts a compound called trimethylamine oxide (TMAO, a kind of fish antifreeze) into trimethylamine (TMA, the stuff that gives old fish that nasty smell). Don't cut into a bluefish until you're ready to marinate it, brine it, or cook it.

Ice it. Cold fish deteriorate more slowly. Because salt water has a lower freezing temperature than fresh, the best way to cool a fish quickly is to create a saltwater slurry by adding seawater to the ice in your cooler. Once you've gotten your well-handled fish home, and you're ready to process:

Brine it. Make a brine of ¾ cup (100 grams) kosher salt, ½ cup sugar, and 2 tablespoons lemon juice per ½ gallon of water. (I specify kosher only because it's what I have in the house. You can use 100 grams of any salt.) Soak the fish for about 18 hours (precise timing isn't critical, and small fillets take less time, large ones more) in the refrigerator.

Dry it. Drain the fillets and pat them dry. Lay them out on racks and let them dry until they form a shiny skin, called a pellicle. This usually takes 2 to 4 hours. The pellicle is supposed to seal in moisture, but I'm not convinced this is true. One of these days, I'm going to do a blind taste test of pellicled vs. non-pellicled bluefish to see if I can tell the difference. In the meantime, though, I don't have the nerve to disregard centuries of fish-smoking advice. I dry the fish, sometimes with the aid of a fan. Once they're dry, I sprinkle them liberally with freshly ground black pepper.

Smoke it. You'll need hardwood chips, charcoal, and a large disposable aluminum roasting pan. First, soak about 2 cups of hardwood chips in water for a few hours. In a kettle grill, start a small chimney of charcoal. When the charcoal's surface is mostly covered in ash, spread the coals in a rectangle roughly the size of the roasting pan in the middle of the grill, leaving the sides clear. Drain the wood chips and spread them over the charcoal.

Punch a bunch of holes in the bottom of the roasting pan and place it upside down over the charcoal and wood chips. The pan prevents any direct heat from reaching the fish, helps keep the fire low, and lets the smoke out through the holes.

(continued)

Put the fillets on the grill and cover it. Adjust the vent so it's almost completely closed, to keep the fire from getting too hot. You're aiming for a temperature of about 150°F. Smoke the fillets until they're cooked through. This should be about 1 hour for ½-pound fillets, 1¼ hours for ¾-pound fillets, and 1½ hours or longer for larger fillets.

It's All About the Bass

Striped bass are a delicious migratory fish. Every year they start the commute from in and around the Chesapeake Bay, where they spawn, and head north as the water warms. Fishermen obsess over the maps, trying to peg the earliest date they might conceivably catch a striper. And not just any striper—a striper big enough to keep. There are limits on fish you're allowed to take, and striped bass have to be at least twenty-eight inches.

The fish come to the south side of the Cape first, and we've caught early ones there. But the epic fishing doesn't start until they make their way to the north side and meet up with one of their favorite foods: mackerel.

Before I'd ever done it, I thought of fishing as one monolithic activity. You get yourself a pole and a line and some bait, then toss the line out there and see what comes up. Might be a perch. Might be a tuna. You hope for the tuna.

It doesn't work that way, of course. For starters, you're fishing *for* something, and you gear up accordingly. If you want trout, you have to fish with something trout find irresistible. In the winter, that's shiners, but irresistibility varies by time of the year, or of the day, or of the tide, by weather conditions or phases of the moon. Sometimes fish feed on the surface, and sometimes wild horses couldn't bring them up out of the depths. Sometimes they eat bugs, and sometimes they eat other fish. Sometimes they're on a juice fast. They are diabolical and independent-minded.

But in the spring, on the north side of the Cape, the stripers are eating mackerel. So to catch a striper, you first have to catch a mackerel.

This is where our friend Bob comes in. Bob grew up around here, fishing. He and his wife, Suzie, spend a lot of time in boats and were two of the first people to help us figure out the lay of the land.

We had already had several people *not* help us figure it out. Cape Codders, particularly those whose families have been here a long time, have a deeply felt sense of history and a commensurate suspicion of newcomers. They call people who come to the Cape from elsewhere "washashores," only they pronounce it *waash-ashaas*. If you are a wash-ashore and you encounter people whose families have been here for four hundred years, you may not find them eager to divulge local knowledge.

I have to say, of all the reasons to turn your nose up at other people, having a family that went absolutely nowhere for four hundred years doesn't seem particularly compelling. But when I point this out, it doesn't tend to make them any more forthcoming.

Bob, though, doesn't mind a wash-ashore, and explained to us how the spring striped bass action works. First you go out into Cape Cod Bay, where the mackerel hang out. You catch a bunch of them, and then you go into the channel that leads from Barnstable Harbor into the bay. You do this on an outgoing tide, because the fish come out with the water.

You put one of the mackerel on your line and drift with the tide until you catch a fish.

Ha!

The first time we tried all this, we were in our boat and Bob was in his, with a few of his friends. We went out to the bay for mackerel and did what Bob told us to do, which was to drop a sabiki rig—a string of tiny little hooks that snag on everything and tangle if you look at them funny, but which are very good at catching mackerel.

Our boats were maybe a hundred yards apart, and we were doing what I thought was the same thing, with what I thought was the same equipment, but Bob was catching mackerel and we weren't.

"What's Bob doing that we're not doing?" Kevin asked me.

I picked up the binoculars, essential fishing equipment for just this purpose.

"He's drinking a beer," I reported.

Kevin rolled his eyes. "But what else is he doing?"

"He's smoking a cigarette."

Great. "But how's he jigging?"

Bob seemed to be doing exactly what we were doing, letting the jig sink and then pulling it up through the water over and over again. The only difference was that when he pulled it up, there was a fish on it. Or several.

And this, ladies and gentlemen, is how fishing superstitions are born.

As a science journalist, I am well schooled on the difference between correlation and causation. I write about it in my *Washington Post* column. I rant about it on social media. I am a full-out correlation/causation crank. And I don't even smoke. But I was absolutely ready to light up a cigarette in the interest of catching a mackerel.

You would be, too, because you're human. And humans, like just about every other animal on the planet, are hardwired for causality. If A happens and then B happens, every fiber of our being will tell us that A caused B. From an evolutionary perspective, it makes perfect sense. If you hear the rustle in the bushes just before the saber-toothed tiger jumps out, you will forever associate the rustle with the tiger and run like hell. Sometimes the rustle will just be a peace-loving antelope, but the downside comes only from *not* running away from the tiger. If you do run away from the antelope, nothing bad happens.

Way back in 1948, behaviorist B. F. Skinner did an experiment in which he put hungry pigeons in cages and sent food pellets down at random intervals. The poor birds ended up believing that whatever they happened to be doing just before the pellet arrived had made it appear, and they kept repeating that behavior. One turned around in the cage (only counterclockwise). One repeatedly stuck its head in the corner. One made pecking motions toward the floor. They'd hop on one leg, bob their heads, or sway back and forth, all because they couldn't believe in randomness.

One lit up a cigarette.

This is the danger of learning from experience. If we did a controlled trial in which some anglers smoke and others don't, keeping all other variables the same, we could answer the question once and for all, but fishing doesn't lend itself to controlled trials. It's too local and too variable, which means that the best way to learn to fish is to actually fish.

Do that, and you'll find that humans don't believe in randomness, either. You will want to duplicate exactly the conditions in which you have caught fish in the past. It's tricky, because some of the conditions *do* matter. It is entirely reasonable to go to the same spot, at the same point in the tide, with wind from the same direction, in the hopes of catching the same kind of fish. But when you start playing the same kind of music, you've descended into superstition.

You will ask yourself, *Can it hurt?* My brother-in-law Marty, an excellent fisherman, is convinced that Boz Scaggs is fish-catching music, and really, it can't hurt. At least until the "Lido Shuffle" starts to get on your nerves.

I know it wasn't the cigarette, but that first mackerel trip was a bust. Not long after, we gave it another shot—this time we took Bob with us and went to the same spot he caught mackerel last time (see!!??). We dropped sabiki rigs down to the bottom and jigged. Nothing.

And then, for a good twenty minutes, a lot more nothing. We cruised around in the general area but marked nothing on the fish-finder. We jigged some more, and more nothing.

"They're either here or they're not." Bob shrugged. If you fish, you have to be philosophical about this and keep jigging.

When you're not catching fish, it feels like you will never ever catch fish again. Catching fish is a pipe dream. Mackerel, you figure, must have gone extinct since Tuesday, when you saw Bob catch them with your own eyes.

And then Kevin got one. And just a couple minutes later, I got one. And then we hit some big schools of them. All three of us would get hit at once, and we'd bring up multiples at a time. I got four fish on one cast. Once we had a couple dozen in the cooler we'd rigged with an aerator to serve as a live well, we headed back to the channel to try for stripers.

The way you do this is by putting the mackerel on your hook and sending it out to swim around where the stripers are. When the striper eats the mackerel, it gets hooked and you reel it in.

When we got to the channel, I picked up my rod and reached for a mackerel.

"Wait a second," Bob said, looking at my setup. "Do you mind if I change the leader?"

The leader is a piece of line between the thing you're fishing with—lure or bait—and the rest of your fishing line. It exists to try and camouflage the fact that the lure or bait is actually attached to something, which could make a fish suspicious. (Except in the case of bluefish, which are too voracious to be suspicious. You use a wire leader so the fish can't bite through it.)

I had a couple feet of transparent monofilament between the hook and the braided line on my reel. Bob dug into his bottomless tackle box and replaced it with transparent fluorocarbon, which looks a lot like monofilament but is much more expensive.

The fish, though, can apparently tell the difference. Then, as now, I was certainly willing to take any tip Bob had to offer. All three of us sent our mackerel out. And we waited.

Our first hit didn't come immediately, but I don't think we waited more than about fifteen minutes. Of course, it was Bob's. I saw him go on the alert, and then I heard the buzz of the drag. He started reeling in his fish—it looked like it was giving him a decent fight—and then all of a sudden the line went slack. He lost it.

I didn't realize how bad this feels until it happened to me, which it did in the next five minutes. And then it happened to Kevin.

Losing a fish is a crushing disappointment. You feel the hit, and your adrenaline starts to flow. The fish takes drag, and you dig in for the fight. And then suddenly it's gone. After the third or fourth fish, I was stomping the deck in frustration.

"I've never lost so many fish in my life," Bob said, and that made me feel a lot better about losing mine.

But just around dusk, things started to change. Bob hooked a fish, and it stayed hooked. He fought it for several minutes and then boated a beautiful thirty-inch striper, easily a keeper.

We went back to the spot he'd hooked it and started drifting with the increasingly rapid outgoing tide. "The end of the tide is usually the best fishing," Bob told us just as he got another bite. This time, thirty-six inches. At least fifteen pounds. A big fish.

When you're live-lining a fish, you disengage the reel and just put your finger on the line so your mackerel can't swim off to Portugal, where there are no striped bass. That quarter inch of fishing line in contact with your fingertip tells you the story of what's going on under the water. At first I had no idea what the story was, but it slowly, over many fishing trips, started to make sense to me. I learned to tell when my mackerel was under threat, because I'd feel jiggy staccato yanks. Sometimes it was a small striped bass just harassing the mackerel, which was too big for it to eat. Sometimes it was a big one likely to be a keeper. Every now and then it's a bluefish, which usually takes a mighty bite and disappears. Surprisingly often, you can often tell the difference by what that quarter inch of line does.

And then your line gets yanked off your finger and starts spooling off your reel at top speed, and you're on. There is just nothing like the *bzzzzz* noise of a fish taking line against the drag.

I have written and read enough fishing stories to realize that unless something unusual happens or you do something stupid, the part about fighting the fish is boring. It's exciting to do, even a little bit exciting to relive as I make the decision not to tell you about it. But if I give you the play-by-play, you will put this book down and go back to something more interesting, like maybe *Principles of Economics* (ninth edition).

Readers, I landed the fish. It was the same size as Bob's—thirty-six inches—and by far the biggest fish I'd ever caught.

The only problem with the trip was that Kevin didn't get a fish, and that was our first indication that a fluorocarbon leader matters; he hadn't switched out his monofilament. Since then, we have had other indications, and I'm almost willing to say it makes a difference, but then I think about Boz Scaggs, and I'm not so sure.

When we got back to the dock, there was a line at the ramp and a boat with a couple of guys from out of town was just ahead of us. They asked us how we did, and we showed them our fish. They said they'd been out for the entire outgoing tide, trolling with umbrella rigs, and hadn't caught a thing; they were hoping for a better day tomorrow.

This is when I learned to fish it forward. Not that Bob called it that. He just did it. He explained that you need to catch mackerel to get the stripers, he told them where to go to look for the mackerel, and he dug into his tackle box for a spare sabiki to give them.

They were extremely appreciative, and I think a bit surprised. Even I was a bit surprised. As Kevin and I had learned to fish, we'd encountered a lot of cagey, tight-lipped fishermen. And I do understand it! You figure out how to fish by fishing, and it's natural to feel like fishing know-how is something you have to earn. Bob believes in niceness and had been generous with us, his friends, but a light went on for me when I saw his generosity with strangers.

We all figure out our home waters, but then, inevitably, go fish somewhere else. If you help the strangers in your local waters, maybe they'll go home and help the strangers in theirs. Sure, there's going to be a little more competition for your local fish, but there really are a lot of fish in the sea. The important part is that the sum total of fishing enjoyment increases. It's kind of an angler's dilemma.

We absolutely do not expect expert fishermen to tell us or anyone else all their secrets. But Kevin and I always fish it forward. If we can help someone, we do. If we ever come to fish your neck of the woods, we're hoping you see it that way, too.

Getting Fresh

When I started eating fish we'd caught ourselves, it was revelatory. The difference between fish just out of the water and other fish is way bigger than I thought it'd be. Sure, I knew freshness was important, but I also bought my fish at one of the best markets in Manhattan, and I figured that was as good as fish gets.

It wasn't.

Come dinnertime, the best thing about the fish you catch is that you just caught it. And fishermen talk about that a lot. What they don't talk about as much is the fish you freeze and take out in February.

Fishing is boom-and-bust. So are most foods you hunt or gather or grow. You have none, until the very moment you have much too much. Which means you can't just get good at using delicious fresh ingredients. You also have to be good at using stuff that's been in the freezer a little too long, and maybe even has a bit of freezer burn. Not to mention stuff that wasn't really that delicious in the first place, like the woody green beans or the sour blackberries. Cooks who go on and on about using only the best, freshest ingredients irritate me. Anyone can make a good meal out of those! It's the not-so-delicious ingredients that separate the wheat from the chaff.

If you take the time and make the effort to procure food first-hand, you will have some big deliciousness wins. Fish is one. Also tomatoes. Wild mushrooms. The turkeys we raised were better than any I'd ever bought. But one of the things that surprised me was that I got the same satisfaction from subpar ingredients. It wasn't the deliciousness that made first-hand foods compelling; it was the first-handedness.

Deliciousness still matters, which is why one of the skills involved in this is abundance management. What do you do when you have much too much? History has endowed us with many choices: you can salt it, you can dry it, you can can it. But modernity has given us the freezer, and that is, for my money, far and away the best choice.

This is why, should you take up fishing, an essential piece of equipment is a vacuum sealer. Air is the enemy, and vacuum-sealed fish lasts longer and tastes better. Even so, the longer it's been in the freezer, the less you should expect from it. Our fish-based dishes get spicier as the winter wears on, and just before this year's fish arrive, I take out the last of the old season, cut them in sticks, and coat them with the same spice mix I use for blackened bluefish sandwiches. Fish tacos reliably signal the start of the new season.

>>>— ALL-PURPOSE TIPS FOR FISHING ON A BOAT —<<<

- **The thing that can ruin a fishing trip faster than not catching fish is seasickness.** I've been there! If you're prone to it, facing into the wind and staring at the horizon (which you definitely should do) may

not be enough. You need better fishing through chemistry: specifically, scopolamine. It's a prescription patch, and you put it behind
your ear the night before you're due to go out in choppy weather (I
use a half, and it's fine for my 140 pounds). It works well for me, and
we've tested it on several friends. It could make you drowsy, but it
should keep nausea at bay.

· **Wear more clothes than you think the weather requires, in layers.**
You might not need them, but if you do, you'll be happy to have
them. And beware of light-colored lightweight clothing, which becomes basically transparent when wet. Underwear is your friend.

· **If you want to stay warm, you have to stay dry, so make sure your out-
ermost layer is waterproof.** And don't forget your hands and feet; bring
gloves and waterproof shoes or boots on all but the warmest days.

· **You can never have too much ice.** It'll look like a lot when you buy
the 20-pound bag in the grocery store, but you'll probably need a
second one. If you fish a lot, you can use those little half-bottles of
water and refreeze them when you're done. Bonus: emergency supply of fresh water.

· **Always bring binoculars.** They can show you what's happening way
over there where the birds are diving, and they are invaluable for
spying on the fishermen who are catching more fish than you.

· **When you finally have a fish on the line, keep your rod tip up.** Face the
fish, and don't try to reel when the fish is taking line. Keep the pressure
on; a slack line will give the fish a chance to shake himself off. And
when you get that fish in the boat, try again in the exact same spot.

· **If you're invited on someone's boat, ask what you can bring.** Offer
food, drink, ice, or volunteer to pick up bait if you're using something
like worms or squid. And it's good to offer to help foot the fuel bill.
And come hell or high water, show up on time.

※≫≫— ≪≪≪

CHAPTER 8

PRACTICING SHELLFISHNESS

I t didn't take long for us to figure out we liked to fish and to be on the water. So much that Kevin decided he wanted to start an oyster farm. We had friends in the business, and he spent a year apprenticing to learn the basics. After that, we happened to be in the right place at the right time to get a lease (which is the hardest part of starting a shellfish farm), and our farm was growing alongside our first-hand food efforts.

The farm is in Barnstable Harbor, and we found ourselves there several times a week. Since we're already there, in a boat, it seemed like a waste of an opportunity not to venture outside the harbor and see if we couldn't get ourselves some lobsters.

It's weird. Look at a lobster and what do you see? A giant bug. The precise relationship between crustaceans and insects is apparently still being debated by taxonomy professionals, but just look at the thing. If you opened your kitchen cabinet and one went scurrying for cover behind the Worcestershire sauce, your first thought would not be *melted butter.* But put it in the ocean, make it a real pain to catch, and it becomes a delicacy up and down the Eastern Seaboard.

Here in Massachusetts, anyone can buy a permit (current cost: $55) and put up to ten pots anywhere there might be lobster. To explain just how eager I was to try this, I will first have to take you back to the Sparks incident.

We were living in New York when Kevin turned forty-five and decided that, for his birthday, he'd like to go to a steakhouse. He doesn't eat steak very often, and when he does, he makes it count by getting the best steak he can find. Sparks, famous not just for steak but for being the restaurant outside of which mobster Paul Castellano was gunned down in 1985, was his choice, and I made a reservation.

While I don't dislike steak, I like lobster better, and Sparks, like many New York steakhouses, had it on the menu. In a big way—the smallest lobster on offer the night we were there was three pounds.

Bring it.

They brought it. I had never eaten a three-pound lobster before, and it was a whole different experience. All those little crevices and crannies that in a lobster weighing a pound and a half have no meat to speak of are well worth excavating in a lobster that weighs three pounds.

Back in 1990, psychologist Mihály Csíkszentmihályi published a book called *Flow: The Psychology of Optimal Experience.* In it, he described flow as a state of complete absorption in a task, of full concentration and engagement. You don't notice time go by, self-consciousness slips away, and all your resources are devoted to whatever it is you're doing.

Csíkszentmihályi should have been there. I started at the claws and worked my way down, cracking every piece of shell, peering into every joint, digging out every morsel. I ate every last piece of that lobster, reducing it to a little pile of shell shards with two antennae sticking out.

Kevin waited until I was almost finished to point out that people were watching. Not outright staring, but sneaking looks over forkfuls of T-bone. I had been so absorbed in the task at hand that I hadn't noticed I'd become a spectacle. Telling the story to friends the next day, Kevin may have used the phrase *Tasmanian devil.*

So yes, I most definitely wanted to try lobstering. And since lobstering starts with lobster traps, we paid a visit to a local commercial lobsterman who cuts down his double-size commercial pots to sell for recreational use when they near the end of their useful life.

Up until then, I had experienced lobster traps only as decor. How heavy can they be, I figured, if they're hanging from the ceiling of a clam shack? Turns out, lobster traps that create ambience aren't the same as lobster traps that trap lobsters. The ambience kind are wood and rope (it's called *line* when it's on a boat, but *rope* when it's on a restaurant ceiling). The trapping kind are wire and concrete. The ones we bought weighed close to forty pounds each.

The traps consist of two "rooms," a kitchen and a parlor. You put some smelly bits of fish in a bag and hang it in the kitchen, which has two holes lobsters can enter through. Once the lobster has eaten his fill, he starts looking for the exit. He doesn't easily find the holes he came in through, because they are suspended over the floor of the trap. Instead, he finds the hole that leads to the parlor. Once he's in there, it's much harder for him to find his way out again.

Loading the ten traps onto the trailer gave us a preview of the work involved in lobstering. Commercial lobstermen and even serious amateurs, use a davit—a metal arm with a pulley that sticks out over the water—to pull up the pots with a motor. We didn't have a davit. Or a motor. So you've got forty pounds that have to be pulled up from the seabed, hand over hand. Factor in the weight of the rope itself, and the seventeen pounds of lobsters you hope to have in the trap, and it starts sounding like a big job. Times ten.

We don't have a track record of being deterred by big jobs, so we brought home our pots and rigged them with the line. We bought buoys and painted them the colors we registered on our permit (blue, white, and orange). We baited them with bluefish detritus—frames, heads, and guts—and piled them on the boat.

I had thought that figuring out where to put the pots would be the tricky part of lobstering, but it's not. You just go out and see where other people put them, and then put yours nearby. For us, that was just north of the buoy that marks the head of the channel into Barnstable Harbor. We'd seen the fields of pots there when we went out for mackerel, and it seemed the obvious choice. We found a spot that was close enough to other pots that we could reasonably expect lobsters (but far enough away that we weren't stepping on any toes), and we dropped our pots in an east-west line, with maybe thirty yards between them.

And then we went home and waited.

The weather had us waiting four days before we got a warm, calm day for our first foray. Kevin navigated to our first pot, and I grabbed the buoy and pulled it on board. Kevin took the first turn and started hauling.

"Is it hard?" I asked.

"Not too bad."

That was good to know, but the fact that it wasn't too bad for Kevin didn't necessarily mean it was possible for me. It has always annoyed me that, although Kevin isn't that much bigger than I am—an inch or two taller and thirty-ish pounds heavier—he is much stronger.

It only took a minute or so for him to get the pot out of the water and onto the gunwale, in clear view. We stared in wonder.

There was a lobster in the trap. An actual lobster. A legal, keeper lobster. On our very first try.

That made pot-hauling easier. I took hold of the rope on our second trap and found that I could pull it up, but not easily. Although I could get it to the surface, I needed Kevin's help to lift it up on the gunwale.

Second trap, second lobster. Astonishing.

All told, we came home with five lobsters weighing a total of about eight pounds, and an understanding of just how much work it was to pull ten pots.

Since then, I've pulled a lobster pot up from the seafloor hundreds of times. We hauled up the early ones by hand, but we eventually wised up and got a davit. And every single time, I stare over the gunwale as it comes out of the water, because it's a little bit of a thrill, every single time, to see what you've pulled up. Cue the laughter from the professionals, who have pulled them up hundreds of thousands of times and probably don't see it quite the same way.

The seafloor is a place that most of us don't get to visit. When you pull up a lobster pot, you get a little diorama of what's going on down there. It's great when there's a lobster. Or two, or even seven (our personal best). But all kinds of other things come up.

We get crabs, including Jonah crabs, which are arguably more delicious than lobsters but are a royal pain to get meat out of. We've gotten small flounder, skate, sea bass, and dogfish, and one tautog that was big enough to keep. We get starfish and sea urchins and sand dollars and some mysterious transparent creatures that have defied my best efforts at identification. We get many, many moon snails. Once we got a beer can, which still has us scratching our heads. Every pot is another opportunity to be surprised.

Often one of the things in the trap is a lobster you're not allowed to take. We can't take a lobster with a carapace less than 3.25 inches (this happens a lot) or more than 5 inches (this has happened exactly twice). We also can't take egg-bearing females, which are easy to identify because lobsters carry their eggs in the nooks and crannies on the underside of their tail. When commercial lobstermen catch an egg-bearing female, they're required to put a little V-notch in her tail fin so she can be identified as a breeder even after her eggs are gone, and we can't take a notched female, either.

It is hard to throw a lobster back. Your brain stem says, "Hey, we caught that fair and square!" and your stomach says, "Hey, that would taste really good!" Luckily, the cerebral cortex has veto power, and mine says, "Hey, we play by the rules, and we want to maintain a sustainable lobster population. Besides, your brain stem can get you in big trouble." Back it goes.

The lobster season begins in spring, and the starting time for the last several years has been determined not by the lobsters but by right whales, who sometimes spend part of their year in Cape Cod Bay. While they're in the area, lobster gear is prohibited, and we're happy to give them free rein until they decide to move along, which is usually in April or May.

It's the spider crabs that mark the end of the season. As soon as you start finding them in your pots, you know the lobsters are mostly gone. I don't know whether they compete for food or that's just the overlap in their migratory patterns, but we take our pots out of the water as soon as we start finding the spiders.

Some years we do better than others, and our seasonal record so far is 151 lobsters. We've hit the daily limit of 15 lobsters several times. We occasionally have so much lobster that we get tired of it. Not lobster *again*.

And lobstering has its downsides. It covers your boat in sea crud and fish guts. If you forget to bring your display buoy, which shows that you are the legit owner of the pots you are pulling, you can get in trouble with the environmental police. You sometimes lose pots to weather, malice, or accidents. You have to take up a corner of the garage with a freezer full of the fish waste you're going to use as bait, and every now and then, somebody will accidentally leave it open, but we won't name names.

But the upside wins, hands down, particularly after you improve your regulation-following and freezer-management skills. Because the upside is lobster, in quantities that you'd be unlikely to buy, even if it were in your budget.

There's something both wholesome and decadent about a gigantic pile of a luxury food you yourself have pulled from the sea. You make a potato salad, grill some corn, and invite your friends. You pass around the lobster crackers and everyone gets to eat as much as they want. A big lobster can be hard to crack and has a tendency to open explosively, so you invariably make an unconscionable mess. But any night you get lobster in your hair is a good night.

⋙ THE PERFECT LOBSTER ROLL ⋘

What's with all the fuss about lobster rolls?

I understand arguing about how to make the perfect chili or brownie or pizza. Those are complicated. Things can go wrong. Reasonable people can disagree. But we all agree on the perfect lobster roll, and any bonehead can make one.

Here's how you do it. Take lobster meat, roughly chopped. Add a small amount of finely chopped onion, maybe with a little celery or fennel. Maybe not. Add just enough mayo to get it to hold together. Serve it on a toasted, buttered roll—a brioche is ideal, but a hot dog roll will do fine. Do not be stingy with the meat.

That's it. If you muck around with it, you will only screw it up.

⋙ ⋘

CHAPTER 9

ONE OF THESE FISH IS NOT LIKE THE OTHERS

As it turned out, the lobster pots gave us more than lobster. They also gave us an excuse to try for one of the fish that anglers look forward to all season: false albacore, which show up around September.

They are a great fighting fish; they're strong and they're fast and they'll battle you as though their life depends on it, which you can't blame them for. They also happen to be the only fish in the tuna family that doesn't taste good. We'd been told that they were downright inedible.

This posed a problem for me. I don't do catch-and-release fishing. Seems to me it's fish torture, pure and simple.

Fishing isn't kind to the fish. The best science we have indicates that they do feel pain, although their nervous systems aren't like ours, so their pain probably isn't, either. But anyone who tells you they don't feel pain is probably trying to justify a fishing habit.

Kevin and I eat animals, and we try to make sure the animals we eat have the best possible lives. We raise them ourselves or buy them from someone else attentive to welfare issues. Or we go out and catch them.

When you fish for food, the downside is suffering and death for the fish and the upside is nourishment for you. When you fish for fun, the downside is suffering for the fish (and sometimes death—the mortality for catch and release is usually estimated at somewhere between 10 and 40 percent), and the upside is . . . a pleasant afternoon.

In my ethical universe, the imperative to feed ourselves justifies killing animals in some circumstances, although this is an idea that will get a lot of pushback, and I think it's something reasonable people can disagree about. But to kill or inflict pain for sport is another proposition altogether, and I don't do it.

Which is why the false albacore were a problem. If you really can't eat them, I really can't fish for them.

But wait! We have lobster pots to catch lobsters, which we eat. Those pots need to be baited with something, and the second-best choice is fish that people don't eat. (The best choice is the leftovers of fish that people do eat, which is what we use most of the time.) False albacore are a dense, fatty, fishy fish, and we figured they'd make excellent lobster bait.

Besides, I wasn't willing to take their inedibility on faith. I was absolutely going to cook one.

We set out to find them on a windy late September day. It was sunny and seasonally warm, but the wind, out of the north, made for a pretty hairy chop. Just as we came out of the protection of West Bay, into Nantucket Sound, the wake from a passing boat came over the bow and drenched us both. I had a waterproof jacket, but nothing over my jeans, so my legs got wet. Kevin was better dressed, and his skin stayed dry.

When you're on a boat (or anywhere, but it's particularly relevant when you're on a boat), the key to staying warm is staying dry. I am susceptible to cold and wasn't happy about getting wet first thing. But we continued on through the channel, Kevin navigating the waves to try and keep them from coming aboard.

For the most part, he was successful, and we didn't get any wetter than we already were, but the conditions were not pleasant. We looked at each other, considering whether we really wanted to do this. And we had just decided that we didn't and turned the boat around when Kevin spotted them.

"They're over there!" He pointed to a spot some fifty yards away, where birds were diving and fins and splashes were making a boil.

All thoughts of going home were abandoned, and we pulled up alongside the fish.

We'd done our homework, which consisted of going to Sports Port, where Amy told us that you catch false albacore with a slim metal lure called a Deadly Dick (and yes, we made all the Deadly Dick jokes, so you don't have to). You cast it over the school and reel it in as fast as ever you can.

It was probably the third cast that Kevin hooked one. I saw the rod bend and heard the *bzzzzz* of the line running out. His eyes widened, and he grinned at me. And then he started reeling.

I have already promised not to tell any more fish-fighting stories, and even though this is a good one, I will fast-forward to getting the fish in the net, and from there into the boat.

A false albacore is a beautiful fish. It's silvery and iridescent, with blue-green markings on its dorsal side and little spots on its belly. And it's solid muscle, much firmer than a bluefish or a striped bass. It's like the difference between a pit bull and a cocker spaniel.

We admired it, and then we killed it with a sharp blow to the head. This one was earmarked for dinner, and then we were fishing for bait.

But a funny thing happened. I found that my heart wasn't in it.

We did go on to catch three more fish. By *we*, I mean Kevin. I struggled with casting a light lure into a heavy wind, and I made too few opportunities for myself to hook a fish. Luckily, my husband was generous enough to let me reel in one of his, so I got something like nine-tenths of the experience.

We kept the first, but we let the next two go. They would undoubtedly have caught us some lobsters, but they were beautiful and unharmed except for a little hole through the lip. It was visceral. Although the lobster pots gave me a reason to take them, I just didn't want to do it. And after we released the second one, I didn't want to fish anymore.

This surprised me. Here we were, smack in the middle of fish that people wait all season for, and I wanted to go home. I had thought I liked fishing because I liked the actual catching of the fish, with an assist from being on the water with Kevin and without the internet. But when I couldn't eat the fish, the enjoyment ebbed away.

Turns out, I don't like catching fish. I like catching food.

We did take that first one home, and I tried to make a meal out of it. I marinated it in lemon juice and mayonnaise, a tactic many people use for de-fishing a fishy fish. Then I broiled it.

It came out of the oven looking like perfectly cooked tuna, and its looks kindled a little flame of optimism that was doused the moment we tasted it. It had a nasty, chewy texture and a very pronounced fishiness. We ate a few obligatory bites and pushed it away.

I have never again gone fishing for false albacore, but fishing for food steadily climbed the charts as one of my favorite activities.

CHAPTER 10

THRILLS AND SKILLS

O nc of thc bcst things about first hand food is that it doesn't break thc bank. You can forage right out your back door, with nothing but enthusiasm. You can start a garden on a shoestring. With a few tools and some ingenuity, you can build a chicken coop that eggs will pay for.

Fishing is the exception. Not at first! If you have a nearby shoreline and some good advice, you can catch enough fish to justify some secondhand fishing gear. But once fishing takes hold of you, boats and trucks are involved, and that's when the spending starts.

Ours started early. By the time I learned that I love to fish, we were already fully boated. We had not just the Eastern, but also a 17-foot Carolina Skiff for the oyster farm, because navigating the oyster flats and transporting equipment required a wide-open flat-bottomed boat. But Kevin was starting to talk about a bigger boat, a boat that could go more places in more weather.

I am on record as believing that Henry David Thoreau was a

self-important gasbag, and *Walden* is unreadable, but he did say, "Beware of all enterprises that require new clothes." As rules for navigating life go, I think this is a pretty good one, and I will say it is a point in first-hand food's favor that new clothes are seldom required. Thoreau never talks specifically about new boats, but I'm pretty sure he would have been against those, too. I know I was balking.

The new boat discussion went on for some weeks, until that day late in the season when we ventured out for bluefish.

We dropped the Eastern in at the ramp, and Kevin parked the truck while I started the boat. Although you do this by turning the key, it's not like a car; there's a whole ritual involved. First, you pump the primer bulb on the fuel line to get some gas in the motor. Then you lift a lever on the controller, but you don't open it all the way or you'll flood the engine. Five-sixteenths is about right.

Then you press the key in three times. Not two, not four. That releases oil to the motor. Last, you sacrifice a goat and offer it up to Vroom, the God of Outboards. There are incantations associated with this, and woe betide you if you get them wrong, but I'd gotten good at getting them right.

And that day, I got them right, but the boat didn't start. It just sputtered and complained. When Kevin came down, he couldn't start it, either. He took the top off the motor, fiddled, tried again, fiddled some more. There were other people waiting to use the ramp, and a little slick of oil was seeping out of the motor.

He finally did get it started, but not before I decided that, if he wanted another boat, he should have another boat. The person responsible for maintaining, troubleshooting, and repairing the boat gets to decide if we get a new one.

After nearly an entire winter's worth of Craigslist-surfing, he found it: a 23-foot Steiger Craft, tricked out for fishing. He also found the 2008 Ford F-250 diesel we'd need to tow it. Thoreau protested from beyond the grave, but I told him to shut up, and also that *Walden* is unreadable.

There was only one problem, and it may have occurred to those of you keeping score. As the boats and trucks accumulated, the Competent Spouse Doctrine had Kevin doing an awful lot of the work around here. In my defense, I will point out that there are some things I am better at, but they are often the boring things. I have spared you the chapter on Vehicle Registration and Insurance, and also the one on Keeping Things White, but those two would have gone a long way to balance out the narrative. If you stick with me, you will also find out that I am in the driver's seat whenever rocks are involved.

That said, as boats became a bigger part of our life, I thought my skill set needed some work. If my Aunt Dag had stood by the Competent Spouse Doctrine, Uncle Frank would have done all the work on the farm. The doctrine really works only when both spouses are reasonably competent. Which is why I decided I would learn to back up a trailer.

I am the first to admit that backing up a trailer is not up there with, say, splicing a gene. But when you're talking about a boat ramp, you're not just backing up a trailer. You're backing up a trailer under pressure.

For starters, a boat ramp is often narrow. The bigger your boat, the less wiggle room you have. Then there are often other people with boats to launch, and they are pointedly looking at their watches.

And then there are the spectators. The rampies. They're the guys (always guys) who just stand around waiting for you to fuck up. Rampies run rampant in coastal towns, and the internet is a testament to their ubiquity. There are a zillion videos of people fucking up at boat ramps because, and only because, someone with a camera is there waiting.

I don't know this for a fact, but I harbor a suspicion, developed over a couple hundred boat launches, that the rampies get particular satisfaction when the person who fucks up is female. Since something like

98 percent of people backing trailers down ramps are male, a woman at the wheel adds a particular frisson of excitement.

At first, I'd back the boat down only if there was no one around, but I got better. And then I got a lot better. And now I'm pretty damn good.

This is a little embarrassing, but I am going to tell you anyway: operating heavy machinery well makes me feel powerful and competent. When I hop into the truck cab in front of all those people and back that boat down quickly and smoothly and perfectly, I am so very big and bad.

Maybe this is just about me, about how pathetically little it takes for me to feel good about myself, but I think there's a human universal buried here somewhere. Pushing your boundaries, learning something new—even something small and mundane—builds you up. Over and over, that's happened to me in our pursuit of food, but there's an extra something satisfying when it's the stuff that men usually do, and motorized.

It's only fair to note that, as good as my boat-backing skills are, Kevin's are still better. Because his skill level on just about everything was originally so much higher than mine, it's been hard for me to catch up, even with practice.

There, is, however, one skill that I have taken as my magisterium where Kevin can't touch me: I can fillet a fish like nobody's business.

Fillet Away

When I try something for the very first time, I often think of an Atul Gawande essay called "The Learning Curve." It's about his surgical training, and how the need to teach new doctors is in tension with the obligation to give the best care. Who's going to be the first patient the new guy operates on? It's got to be somebody, or there will never be new doctors.

But it's also about how you learn physical skills. It's not about magic hands, or any other kind of innate ability. Surgeons, he wrote, "believe in practice, not talent."

He describes how he learned to insert a central line, how he struggled and made mistakes and lost confidence and then, one day, he got it right. "That's the funny thing about practice. For days and days, you make out only the fragments of what to do. And then one day you've got the whole thing."

I know that comparing this to learning to fillet is a bit of a stretch. The stakes are worlds apart—live human versus dead fish—but the feeling is exactly what he describes. You watch the videos of other people doing it, you sharpen your fillet knife, and you make the first cut from behind the pectoral fin up to just behind the head. Then down the top ridge of the fish, the first step to releasing the fillet. Then breathe a sigh of relief that you're not Gawande because you just punctured a lung.

From the very first fish I filleted, it mattered to me that I did it well, and initially I couldn't articulate why. The worst that could happen was that I could make a hash of it and end up with mangled fillets. And who cares? But I did.

Fish were my first foray into turning an animal into something you could cook and serve for dinner, or vacuum-seal and freeze, and it has been the same with every bird I've parted out, every deer I've broken down. I have to do it as well as I possibly can.

I know a lot of hunters, homesteaders, and fishermen who feel the same, and the shorthand is that it's a sign of respect for the life taken. For me, that's not quite right, and I understand why people ridicule the idea that you don't respect a life by taking it. The animal is dead, and beyond respect.

Butchering well, and wasting nothing, is instead a way to say that the whole enterprise is important, that I don't take a life lightly. That life matters, and the care I take is both a mark of the seriousness of the decision to take it and a reminder to care as much next time.

Of the things we do, fishing has one of the longest learning curves. Every year, we've tried to expand our repertoire, tackling a new species or a new area or a new technique, and I'm happy to report that I've learned to fillet black sea bass, tautog, fluke, cod, haddock, scup, and bonito, along with the usual bluefish and striped bass. At the peak of squid season, when I've had a little practice, I can clean a squid in twenty seconds. When I look at the freezer full of fish that takes us into the winter, I feel pretty good about what we've learned, but when I talk to friends who are way better than we are at fishing, I still feel like a complete amateur.

And that's exactly why we can't go around comparing ourselves to people who are truly expert. It's true of fishing, but it's also true of everyday skills like cooking. For nearly all of human history, we bumbled through almost everything, learning from family and neighbors and developing skills as we went along. Progress is when you can do it better than you did last year.

If you want to try your hand at fishing, join the fishing community. Head down to the bait store. Talk to Amy or anybody in the store—I guarantee you they're interested in fishing. Buy some basic equipment. And then just go get a line wet.

PART IV

CHAPTER 11

SEE SALT FORM.
FORM, SALT, FORM!

L et me take you back to our Winter of Shellfish.

After we decided on New Year's Day that we would eat at least one thing we grew, hunted, or gathered every day, it was all clams all the time. We were getting very tired of clams, and also of cold.

That first winter made me understand where the expression "hardy New England stock" came from. In a population shift dating back to the Pilgrims, all the wimps took to the hills after their first February. What was left were the people who were willing to put their underwear on in October and take it off in April.

I was beginning to see the merit of that system. In the dead of winter, when the temperature outside is in single digits and the temperature inside tops out at brisk, it's hard to muster the courage to take a shower—or engage in any other activity that involves removing your base layer. My admittedly anemic collection of lacy little La Perla confections was out of the rotation, displaced by more practical options. You know the thrill is gone when you choose underwear that keeps you warm and doesn't show the dirt. (Luckily, the same landscape that keeps us clothed all winter works in reverse in the summer, when we can skinny-dip in perfect privacy. Unless our neighbors have very powerful binoculars. Like ours.)

On one ridiculously cold day, Kevin and I were sitting in our living room, layered up and grateful for our woodstove, trying to come up with a new, exciting way to cook clams. The stove can heat a space twice the size of our house, so when we put it through its paces, our living room can get very warm. Normally, we don't let that happen both because we're trying to be hardy New England stock and because we don't want to waste fuel, but on this particular day, we were feeling dispirited and profligate, and we both really needed a shower. We put it through its paces.

Like all people who heat with wood, we maintain humidity by keeping a cast-iron pot with a lattice top filled with water on top of the stove. The stove was so hot I could see little tendrils of steam rising out of it. Suddenly and inexplicably, I had an idea.

"What would happen," I asked Kevin, "if we put seawater in that pot?"

He looked at the pot. "It would evaporate?" He asked it as a question not because he was unsure whether it would, but because he was unsure why I was asking.

"And after that happened, wouldn't we be left with sea salt?"

It was a rhetorical question, because of course we would. And so began one of the most surprising of our first-hand food enterprises. Surprising, even though we knew, going in, exactly what would happen.

Salt is essential for human life, and all of it originates from the sea. Even the stuff that comes from salt mines was at some point in planetary history dissolved in water. Calling something *sea salt* rather than just salt doesn't tell you much other than the recency with which it was wet, and that someone probably wants to charge a premium for it.

This makes no sense at all, given that sea salt is all around those of us who live near a coast, free for the taking. The only problem, of course, is extracting it from the water, a process that requires energy. Since energy is expensive and salt, even sea salt, is cheap, this is usually a losing proposition. But we were already in the evaporation business.

Kevin wasn't sold. "So we drive to the ocean, schlep the water back here, store it in the house, keep filling the pot with it, and end up with, what, three tablespoons of salt, retail value seven cents?"

"I think it'll be more than that," I said, with more confidence than I felt. How much salt is in seawater, anyway?

A quick google told us that seawater is about 3.5 percent salt by weight, which means that each liter of seawater should yield thirty-five grams, about an ounce and a quarter. A gallon should yield nearly five ounces, a significant haul.

Kevin didn't believe it.

"I don't believe it," he said.

But he kind of did believe it, because he believes in math. It was just that the math didn't jibe with his gut sense of how much salt we'd get. And every last one of us, when math doesn't jibe with gut, instinctively goes with gut. To go with math requires that your brain step in to override your gut, something your brain is generally unwilling to do. In this case, though, Kevin's brain wanted to sort this out, and so he was in.

To get the salt out of the water, you first have to get the water out of the ocean. I donned my waders and Kevin and I put our largest manageable container—a four-gallon stainless steel stockpot—in the back of the truck. We headed out to Sandy Neck, a barrier beach on the north side of the Cape, facing Cape Cod Bay.

I was grateful for the cold, because it meant there were only a couple of people there to watch the spectacle of a woman in waders heading into the surf with a giant pot. I would like to emphasize the word *surf* here. This was no millpond; there were two-footers coming in. And if you think a two-foot wave is a walk in the park I will ask you to hold your smirk until you, too, have waded into two-footers trying to fill a giant pot with seawater.

After several inept swoops that bagged a cup or so of water and several pounds of sand, I finally caught a wave in the sweet spot and filled the pot.

I was not sure then, and am not sure now, that this is legal. I suspect there is a statute somewhere on the Massachusetts books that says that you're not allowed to remove anything from the Commonwealth's beaches—no water, no sand, no flotsam, no jetsam. But nobody stopped us, and we took it home to evaporate.

To maximize evaporation, you want to maximize surface area, and we thought the best vessel for this experiment would be our Le Creuset cast-iron roasting pan. The iron would retain heat and the 10×14-inch surface would turn our water to salt relatively quickly. I thought the enamel would prevent corrosion, but I was a little worried about the fate of my favorite roasting pan, which I often use for more conventional purposes. Even so, I was willing to chance it in the interest of science, and also as something that would qualify for our one-a-day challenge that wasn't clams.

When we got home, we poured the water through a coffee filter to remove at least some of the sea schmutz—scraps of seaweed and various unidentifiable floating objects—and put the filtered water into the roasting pan. We stoked the stove, and we waited.

Watching water evaporate should be exactly as exciting as watching paint dry; it's the same process. Which is why I can't account for the time Kevin and I spent standing around the stove, staring at the water, waiting for the salt to materialize. When the level went down, we refilled it and watched some more. Again, thanks to the internet, I knew that water will dissolve 38 percent of its weight in salt before no more will dissolve. Since the salt in seawater is about one-tenth of that maximum, I figured the salt would start precipitating out when the water was reduced to one-tenth its volume.

You will be happy to hear that the immutable principles of chemistry worked as expected, and when we were down to our last quart and a half, we began to see a thin film of salt form on the surface. That's when the excitement reached fever pitch!

The water continued to evaporate, and we started pushing the salt to the edges of the pan. Within twenty-four hours of the formation of the first crystals, we had a pan full of beautiful snowy white sea salt. It was just over a pound, which translates to 35 grams per liter, exactly 3.5 percent by weight.

I shouldn't have been surprised. I'm pretty good at math, and this was basic arithmetic. But that beautiful pile of salt was the next best thing to creating something out of thin air. You take water out of the ocean, put it on your woodstove, and end up with something people put in froufrou little containers and sell at the same per-pound price as wild-caught salmon. We were mesmerized by a completely mundane process we could predict with perfect accuracy.

We weren't the only ones; it proved as compelling to other people as it was to us. Here's this process that requires absolutely no experience or expertise. You just get some seawater and evaporate it. Over the next few years we'd expand our fishing territory, raise various kinds of livestock, and learn to hunt, but people who followed along with our adventures often thought that our saltworks was our most interesting undertaking. It caught the fancy of my friend Elspeth, a writer and reporter for our local NPR station, WCAI. Not only did she do a radio spot on our enterprise, she and her husband tried it at home. "We've been keeping the house at 110 degrees so we can make more of it," she told me.

Not long after that, I was invited to speak at a gardening forum at Cape Cod Community College. "I know you do a lot of things," the organizer told me, "but make sure you talk about the salt."

But . . . but . . . I learned how to use a *hammer*! Don't you want to hear about *that*?

Not really, no.

"Is it safe to eat?" is the question we get most. And the science journalist in me is happy to tell you that it is! No pathogen can survive in salt, which is why it's used to preserve food. Although it's possible for sea salt to be contaminated with things like heavy metals or microplastics, it's virtually impossible to eat so much salt that they're a genuine risk. There's also no reason that DIY salt would be more dangerous than salt from other sources. If you're worried about risk, don't text and drive; your salt is fine.

Once they're reassured about safety, people without woodstoves often ask if they can just boil the water to get the salt. Which of course they can, but it's an awful waste. People without woodstoves should instead go solar. Wait for summer, rig up a shallow container that gives you lots of surface area, and leave it in full sun. It will take longer, but it will be just as miraculous.

That first winter, we made pounds of the stuff. And occasionally I let it count as our food of the day, but that felt like cheating. As the weather warmed, and our salt production waned with our woodstove use, I started scouring the landscape for something, anything, green and edible that wasn't a goddamn clam. It was way too early for the garden, but by mid-March the first wild plants were poking up through last year's leaves.

CHAPTER 12

IT GROWS BY THE WAYSIDE

When it comes to green edible wild things, Euell Gibbons wrote the book: *Stalking the Wild Asparagus*. Even though it was published in 1962, it's still the book I'd start with if you want to learn to forage. And if you don't want to learn to forage, it may make you reconsider.

What has made first-hand food compelling to me is that it feels like it scratches a primordial itch to feed ourselves, and Gibbons thinks so, too: "Don't we sometimes feel that we are living a secondhand sort of existence, and that we are in danger of losing all contact with the origins of life and the nature which nourishes it?"

Yes, Euell, I believe we do. And I'm with you in finding wild edibles to be an antidote. I don't always agree, though, on just what constitutes "edible."

When we experimented with perennial greens (the nice name for wild plants somebody's trying to convince you to plant in your garden), we learned a little bit about how plants protect themselves. When a plant doesn't have a human to take care of it—to give it water and fertilizer, and to protect it from insects and fungi—it has to fend for itself. Deliciousness is not in its best interest; the smart plant is bitter, woody, hairy, or poisonous.

I have a grudging admiration for those plants. They're scrappy survivors, depending on nothing and no one. They make it through cold years and wet years, hot years and dry years. They grow unassisted in the cracks in the sidewalk, the gutters of your house, and even Carver coarse sand. If humans suddenly disappeared from the planet (and it could happen), chickweed would carpet the earth in no time.

One of wild plants' strategies for world domination is to get a head start. Early in spring, when most of us haven't begun thinking about gardens because we're still thinking about whether it's time to take off our underwear, wild plants are already well on their way. It is when those wild plants first start poking through the still-cold earth that I ventured out, armed with Gibbons and optimism, to find something good to eat.

The problem with early spring foraging is that when they're just coming up, all plants look mighty similar. You find a little shoot with a few leaves, and it doesn't seem to look like any of the plants in *Stalking the Wild Asparagus* or any other field guide, and you have no idea whether it's safe to eat. This is when you resort to the Universal Edibility Test.

This is really a thing. Honest, look it up. And when you can't identify a plant, it sounds like an excellent thing to try—at least until you find out what actually goes into it. It's not like a litmus test or a pregnancy test, where you just dip a stick into something and watch it turn color. The Universal Edibility Test involves first pressing a molecule of the substance to your lips and then waiting. If nothing bad happens, then you press it to your tongue and wait some more. Then you chew, but don't swallow. Then you chew and swallow. Then you go through the cycle with two molecules. And of course you have to do this with every part of the plant separately. The stem could be safe, but the leaf is a whole different story.

The advantage to the Universal Edibility Test is that it does, indeed, tell you whether a plant is edible. The disadvantage is that it takes seventeen years. There is some consolation in knowing that you'll be able to pass this information on to your grandchildren, but in order to be useful, the Universal Edibility Test needs some serious streamlining.

My modified Universal Edibility Test, which I am emphatically not recommending to other people, is to just taste the damn thing, and figure if it tastes good enough to eat, it probably won't kill me.

Disclaimer here in BIG LETTERS: I do not use this test for fruit, which can taste good but be poisonous, and I use a modified version for only the subset of mushrooms whose lethality I can rule out (more on that later).

When it comes to leaves, though, poisonous compounds almost always taste terrible, and I'm willing to chance a leaf or two of anything that tastes good. If nothing bad happens, I can put it on the menu.

This is all talk, of course, until you actually find a wild plant that tastes good. That first spring I tasted scads of nascent little nasties, and they were all, as predicted, some combination of bitter, woody, hairy, and poisonous. I found two—two!—plants worth eating, and wonder of wonders, I could identify both. One barely counts because it was dandelion greens, which any child can identify. For the second, there was enough of the plant above ground to make a positive ID from a guidebook. If you have access to daylily shoots, clean them thoroughly and sauté them lightly; they taste like a very mild scallion.

Also delicious enough that Gibbons put it in his book title is wild asparagus. I know there is some on Cape Cod because every summer I see the same patch of overgrown fronds near one of the south-side beaches. Unfortunately, when I go in the spring, which is when the tender green shoots should be coming up, I can never find it in the underbrush. This year, I'll drop a pin.

Other than that, the only wild greens in my part of the world that are worth the trouble are in the onion family. And you don't even have to taste them to identify them; they all smell like onions. Chives, ramps, and any kind of wild garlic or onion are good, and some come up quite early in the spring.

Gibbons has a different and vastly more inclusive definition of good. I'd go so far as to say he stretches the limit of edibility to its breaking point, which, if you read between the lines, he basically admits. "Some [wild foods] require special treatment and skillful preparation to make them acceptable to a discriminating taste." That category includes plants that must be boiled for hours before they're palatable (acorns), need to be used in very small quantities (cattail flour), or are simply not appreciated by the "average palate" (sassafras paste). If you find any of these unappealing, it could be your own fault. "Learn to appreciate new flavors," he admonishes.

Although Gibbons undoubtedly ate and probably relished plants I can't warm up to, I have a real fondness for anyone who'll try absolutely anything—any plant, anytime, anywhere. And if it's no good, he'll boil it for a while and try it again. If the leaf's no good, he'll try the root. If all else fails, he'll make an infusion.

And that's why, when I figured I'd exhausted the springtime greenery, I was willing to follow him down another path. It helped that alcohol was involved.

While the first dandelion greens come out in March or April, there aren't dandelion flowers in quantity until May. When they started to bloom, I kept my eyes open for a good spot for picking. *Good*, in this case, means dense with dandelions, away from heavy car traffic, and not on the front lawn of anyone with a shotgun and a short temper.

I found the perfect field on an Audubon preserve a few miles east of us. When the dandelions were in their glory, if dandelions can be said to be glorious, Kevin and I went out and snipped off two gallons of dandelion flowers. For the record, two gallons is a lot of dandelion flowers. Dandelions have the chutzpah to grow close to the ground, and harvesting them means a lot of stooping, bending, and squatting. If you know people with young backs you can enlist for this job, definitely enlist them.

We took our haul home and left the flowers outside to give the insects a chance to escape; neither they nor we wanted them involved. Then we started the winemaking process.

There are many recipes for dandelion wine, but most of them are similar to Euell Gibbons's. You steep the flowers in water for a few days, then drain them and bring the liquid to a boil with sugar, citrus juice, and other flavoring agents. Cool it down and add yeast. Let it ferment and then age. Different recipes call for different quantities and timing, but that's the basic process.

Here's Gibbons's version:

1. Pour one gallon of boiling water over one gallon of dandelion flowers. Steep for three days.

2. Strain out the flowers and add a small piece of chopped ginger, the zest and juice of three oranges and a lemon, and three pounds of sugar to the liquid.

3. Boil the mixture for twenty minutes. Let it cool to lukewarm and add a package of yeast. Cover loosely and leave in a warm place for a week.

4. Strain into a gallon jug, cap loosely, and keep in a dark place for three weeks. Then decant and cork tightly. Wait at least six months. Drink.

This raises an important question. If you're making dandelion wine, what's with the oranges? This is a recipe for stone soup.

Remember the story? It's a folktale about a man who swans into town with a pot and a stone, promising soup. He boils up the stone and then muses that the soup might taste even better with an onion. And some carrots. And maybe a chicken. He cons all the ingredients out of the townspeople, who then marvel at what delicious soup a stone makes.

Going into this, I suspected that the whole dandelion part—which involves hours of backbreaking labor and many, many ants—was just inserted into the recipe to build character, and the first steps did nothing to disabuse me of this notion. If you ever encounter dandelions that have been steeped in water for a few days, you will be tempted to throw the whole mess out the back window. The flowers are gray and waterlogged, and they smell like lettuce that's been in the fridge too long.

I looked at this vegetal mess and kept thinking how much nicer orange juice would be. The only reason we thought it might possibly turn into wine is that it has, for other people, gazillions of times over the course of wine-making history.

It's hard to picture the first couple who tried it. I imagine them peering skeptically at the soggy, smelly mess in their crock. He says, "That doesn't smell very good." And she says, "If this was okay to do, wouldn't other people do it?"

Things looked up when we strained out the flowers and threw them out the back window. Once you add the ginger, orange, lemon, and sugar, it starts resembling a beverage. We boiled it, added the yeast, and left it to bubble away.

A few days later, we realized we had the kind of problem you end up with when you don't read the recipe to the very end: we needed jugs to put the finished product in. Specifically, two one-gallon glass jugs. Hop on the internet, and a one-gallon glass jug will set you back between $5 and $15, delivery date uncertain.

Right down the street, though, we could buy them for $12.99 each. The only catch was that they were filled with Carlo Rossi Chablis.

The science of enology has come a long way in the last couple of decades, and cheap wine isn't nearly as bad as it used to be. A little seltzer, a little ice, and it was absolutely drinkable. But two more of our rules to navigate life—don't waste and don't drink plonk in large quantities—were definitely in tension for a while there.

You have no idea how many things can be cooked in wine until you have a bathtub full of a kind you're too embarrassed to serve to your friends. A few stews later, we'd solved the problem and stocked the freezer. We promptly removed the incriminating labels from the jugs, strained the bits of fruit out of the dandelion wine, and poured it in.

Ideally, at this stage, you rig the jugs with a fermentation trap, a gizmo that allows the carbon dioxide produced by what fermentation is still going on to escape without letting any air in. A bona fide fermentation trap is a glass or plastic tube with a big bend and three bulbs, and you can buy it from people who sell winemaking supplies. Alternatively, you can rig a tube through a cork and run it into a water bath.

Or you can just put a balloon over the jug mouth. Guess what we did.

There was a little left over, though, which of course we had to drink. It tasted—surprise!—of orange and lemon and ginger. It had a faint effervescence and a distinct alcoholic edge. But I have to admit that it also had a pleasant note of green weediness.

After a year, it tasted kind of like that, but mellower, and it improved as it aged. Over the years, we've made five or six vintages, and I am persuaded that the dandelions are after all an important part of the recipe.

They are also the source of the satisfaction. Dandelions are arguably the most mundane plant going. The fact that they're everywhere in quantity is a royal pain if you're maintaining a lawn, but a windfall if you're making wine. We tend to prize anything that's rare—scarcity is literally the only reason that gold is expensive—and it feels a tiny bit subversive to find value in something almost literally as common as dirt.

But it's also just plain satisfying to collect something that carpets the ground and turn it into something to drink—or eat. Which is why, in the fall, our thoughts invariably turn to acorns.

CHAPTER 13

ACORNUCOPIA

I grew up in the Northeast, so it's a little embarrassing that it wasn't until I was in my forties that it occurred to me that acorns were food. I knew acorns were nuts, and I knew nuts were food, but I didn't connect the dots until we had pigs.

Pigs love acorns. The first time we had them, we watched them scarf up the ones that fell into their pen (it was 2,000 square feet in the woods, and there were quite a few), and then we started collecting them from other parts of the property.

It was a win for everyone. The pigs got acorns, and the people who'd be eating the pigs got acorn-finished pork, the stuff the legendary Iberian ham is made of. In Iberia, though, they bring the pigs to the acorns; they let them loose in the forest to forage for themselves. Although this is the sensible way, we didn't think our neighbors would go for it. We also had some rather unfortunate experiences with the difficulties involved in getting pigs from outside the pen to inside the pen, so we decided to bring the acorns to the pigs.

It was a great plan in theory. The problem is that acorns are small and pigs are large. If you've ever wondered just how many acorns a pig can eat, I'm here to tell you that it's a gazillion. The acorns that fell on our driveway were barely more than an afternoon snack.

I'd almost resigned myself to the idea that acorns would have to be an occasional treat when Al and Christl showed up one day with a big box.

You will remember them as the people with the wonderful garden, but their resourcefulness didn't stop there. They had found a huge oak on some conservation land near their house, and the box was filled with acorns. And they weren't those scrawny hard-shelled red oak acorns that fall on our driveway; they were huge smooth thin-shelled white oak acorns.

Even before that day, the pigs held Christl in high regard. She brought them treats regularly, and there was one particular visit involving bagels and sour cream that I was pretty sure stuck in their memory. But after the acorns, they put a picture of Christl up on the wall of their house, with an altar and a candle. They worshipped her.

Until that big box, I'd had no idea that acorns grew so big or could be acquired in such quantity. Christl drew a map to the tree responsible for her haul, and Kevin and I went to visit it a couple days later.

That tree turned out to be on the edge of a small woods populated with white oak, and I was astonished at the sheer volume of nuts. They were everywhere, and we could fill a five-gallon bucket in just a few minutes.

Over a period of about a month, Kevin and I collected a couple hundred pounds of acorns. There were so many that even though we filled garbage cans with them, there was still plenty left for the wildlife.

That's what got me thinking. I was very focused not just on feeding us from first-hand food sources, but on trying to make those foods account for a significant portion of our diet. As our efforts expanded, I tracked what percent of our caloric needs we were meeting. And by *tracking*, I mean keeping a list on the back of an envelope and adding up the calories. That exercise, approximate as it was, taught me just how hard it was to make a meaningful dent.

The nutmeats you can get out of a pound of acorns come to about 1,000 calories. A garbage can full of acorns probably weighed fifty pounds. Given that I'd dug and fished and scrounged for foods with woefully pitiful calorie counts, that was awfully tempting. And it was *right there*.

People absolutely, positively can eat acorns. They've been eating them on this continent since way before Europeans arrived. But there's a catch.

Next acorn season, find yourself an acorn, crack it open, and taste it. Nasty, right? It's bitter and tannic, because it's chock-full of tannins, which are reputed to be bad for you. We don't have a good handle on precisely which bad things will happen to you if you eat too many tannins, because they taste so unpleasant that people are unlikely to do that on their own, and a study that force-fed people raw acorns to gauge the health effects would be frowned upon by the oversight board. And some tannins are probably fine, because we happily drink them in wine and nobody has ever presented with tannin overdose from, say, a 1998 Mouton Rothschild.

However, if you don't get some of those compounds out of the acorns, they will be inedible, rendering the uncertainties of tannin science moot. The good news is that there's a straightforward way to remove them. The bad news is it involves soaking them in water over and over and over again. Instructions for doing this recommend that you soak them, drain the water, and soak them again until the water no longer turns brown.

I am suspicious of instructions like this. Anyone who's ever tried to rinse rice "until the water runs clear," which is what they always tell you to do, knows that the water never actually runs clear. It just gets progressively less cloudy until you can't take it anymore.

Standard-issue acorn-processing instructions offer you two choices: the boiling method and the cold-water method. For the boiling method, you're supposed to bring a pot of water to a boil on the stove and soak the acorns until the water turns the color of tea. While you're doing that, you bring a second pot of water to a boil. Take the acorns out of the tea, put them in the clean boiling water. Dump the tea, refill the pot, and bring it to a boil again.

Repeat until the water is clear or hell freezes over, whichever comes first.

Also, since I just finished telling you I thought boiling water endlessly to make sea salt was wasteful, I can't in good conscience recommend boiling water endlessly to make acorn flour.

There is a better way. It's the cold-water way, which still involves changing the water regularly, but takes much longer. Luckily, we all have an appliance that can do that work for us: every time you flush the toilet, the tank empties and refills.

Hear me out! I know you're balking. Even my mother balked, and she is generally in favor of unconventional problem-solving approaches and is also not remotely fastidious. But everything icky that happens in a toilet happens downstream from the tank. The water that fills your tank is the same water that fills your bathtub. It is perfectly fine. And besides, you're going to be exposing those acorns to heat afterward, so any stray pathogen will meet its maker.

We broke out the nutcrackers.

I sure wish our toilet could handle that step, too. Shelling acorns is a tedious business. They don't pop cleanly out of their shells, like hazelnuts or almonds. They cling and crumble and generally give you a hard time. But we managed about two pounds of meats.

I put them in a laundry bag and popped them in the toilet tank.

For days, I watched the water get less brown with every flush. After a week, the bitterness was gone.

The acorns were still tannic, though, so I was not optimistic about turning them into something delicious. I like a nice tannic cabernet as much as the next guy, but tannins in baked goods are not quite the same.

Truth be told, I probably like a nice tannic cabernet considerably more than the next guy, unless the next guy is Kevin, or maybe Robert Parker, and I still couldn't picture them as a plus in a bread.

But, having come this far, I wasn't going to give up. I dried them in a slow oven and ground them to bits in my turbocharged Vitamix blender, which could puree the furniture if it had to.

My acorn flour neither looked nor smelled appetizing. It was a dark gray-brown, and it had a kind of wet-dog smell mixed in with its nuttiness (and don't start with your theories that things that come out of a toilet tank sometimes do end up smelling bad because that had NOTHING TO DO WITH IT). If it hadn't taken so much work to get it to this stage, I might have thrown up my hands and given it to the pigs.

Many of our projects have this feature. They take a long time, they're many steps, and sometimes the only thing that keeps you going is the fact that you've already invested too much time and effort to turn back. I started looking at recipes.

Most acorn recipes fall into one of two categories. Either they're so heavy on the acorns that they can't possibly be good or—and this is the bigger category—they're so light on the acorns that you may as well leave them out. An "acorn cake" recipe that calls for three cups of flour and a tablespoon of acorn is just so passive-aggressive.

I turned to Hank Shaw, who's been in the business of turning wild food into delicious things for many years and is very good at it. His website, Hunter Angler Gardener Cook, has a number of acorn recipes, and I went with flatbreads. The flour-to-acorn ratio was 3:1, which struck me as reasonable.

My dough didn't look much like his. Some of my acorn pieces were a little too big, and they turned almost black—which made the dark ball of dough look like mocha chip ice cream, which reminded me that there are lots of delicious things in the world, so why am I making acorn flatbreads again? But I let it sit for several hours, and then cut off a piece, rolled it flat, and fried it a couple of minutes on each side.

I took it out of the pan and looked at it suspiciously. It was dense and dark, but it had a few bubbles in it and was crispy around the edge. I cut two pieces off and handed one to Kevin. We each took a tentative bite.

I am increasingly convinced that, in all kinds of experimentation, low expectations are your friend. If you go in thinking you're going to impress Gordon Ramsay, it will all end in tears. But if you go in thinking that your pigs are gonna love this, there's nowhere to go but up.

It wasn't bad. It wasn't bad at all. It had a nice chew and a nutty flavor. And no wet dog (SEE!). I served it with some goat cheese and sea salt, and I will go so far as to say it was tasty. I decided not to give the remaining acorn flour to the livestock, and we kept making flatbreads until we used it up.

Turning acorns into food is well worth doing because it will forever change how you look at them. I literally cannot walk past an acorn without thinking that somebody—person or animal—should eat it. Often, of course, an animal will. But every fall, untold tons of them go to waste, becoming neither oak trees nor food.

My appreciation for acorns is visceral at that level, but it's really only theoretical when it comes to bothering to do the work to end up with something almond flour can do better, and without effort on my part. Sometimes things that are well worth doing are only well worth doing once, and we never again turned acorns into flour. But whenever we have livestock that likes them (chickens and turkeys do, too), we go to the conservation land with the white oaks and collect buckets of them. When high-quality food literally falls out of trees, it seems a shame to waste it.

There is, however, one kind of wild food that is absolutely, positively, unequivocally better than any store-bought wannabe.

Of course there's a catch there, too.

CHAPTER 14

INSERT FUNGUS JOKE HERE

I understand why some foragers draw the line at mushrooms. The upside is a tasty side dish and the downside is an excruciating death. Why risk it when you can grow several kinds of excellent mushrooms at home? That's where I was until the Melody Tent incident.

Up to that point, I'd directed almost all my fungal energy into our home-grown shiitakes; my forays into wild mushrooms had been tentative and timid. I'd brought home a few of the easily identifiable kind—boletes, which have pores instead of gills—but found them to be slimy and unpleasant. Then, right on our own property, I found a lovely cluster of honey mushrooms (identifiable by their light brown color, the tiny little hairy speckles on the cap, and the big clusters they grow in). I cut them up and sautéed them in butter, intending to make a pasta sauce. When I added the wine, though, about fifty little white worms floated to the surface.

That put me off mushrooms for a while, and it has put me off honey mushrooms for good and all.

But then one brisk fall day we were running errands in Hyannis, which is what passes for a booming metropolis here on Cape Cod. We were driving by the Melody Tent, a music venue that's been there since I was a kid. It was closed for the season and its parking lot was empty.

"Did you see that?" Kevin asked as we drove by at about 40 miles per hour.

No, of course I didn't see it. I didn't see it because I'm not the one with bionic peripheral vision.

In New York, Kevin worked on the floor of a commodity exchange. The pits where they used to trade don't really exist anymore, since online trading has displaced them, but back in the day, they were crowded and loud.

If you've ever visited a trading floor (or watched the 1983 movie *Trading Places* with Eddie Murphy—Kevin was an extra!), you know how chaotic it looks. It's people, nearly all of them men, standing on bleacher-like rings, yelling and signaling to one another. The coffee pit, where Kevin spent most of his career, was small: about thirty-five people in a twenty-foot circle. The crude oil pit was much bigger, with a couple hundred traders.

If you didn't know better, you'd think they were all angry. And most of the time, at least a few of them probably were, but that wasn't what was going on. It's just that the features of open outcry trading—raised voices, wide-armed gestures—are in ordinary life the hallmarks of anger, so that's what it reads as.

Being angry, in fact, doesn't help at all. What they had to be was focused. Each trader had to be aware of everything that was happening in the pit—who was selling, who was buying, at what price. That meant tracking the entire ring.

Who knew that commodity trading was excellent training for mushroom hunting?

Kevin is always aware of what's going on in the periphery. He's the one who sees the rabbit run under the bush over there on the left, or the kid steal the Snickers bar down the aisle on the right. "Did you see that?" he'll ask me, and I'll look—but it's always too late.

Unless it's a mushroom. They don't move very fast. The one he spotted at the base of an oak tree just next to the Melody Tent parking lot stayed right where it was as we turned around and went back for it.

The thing was multilobed and gray-brown, the size of a bicycle helmet. It smelled good. I took a tentative nibble and it tasted good, too. No bitterness at all. We took it home and broke out our collection of mushroom guidebooks.

The maddening part of mushroom foraging is the infrequency with which the mushroom in the woods (or the parking lot) looks like a mushroom in the guidebook. There is so much variety, so many close relatives, that specific identification is often difficult. In this case, though, we got a direct hit: it was a hen-of-the-woods, also known as maitake.

That was the mushroom that lit up my enthusiasm for wild mushrooms. It's hard to describe flavors in general, and I find mushroom flavors to be particularly elusive. I want to say our hen-of-the-woods was earthy but like wine is earthy, not like earth is earthy. Although, come to think of it, it is like earth is earthy. But in a nice way. It was meaty and umami-rich and huge. It made the single best mushroom soup ever to grace our dinner table.

Which brings us to one of the problems with mushroom hunting that no one ever talks about: it's hell on your carbon footprint.

Think back to B. F. Skinner's pigeons, the ones who thought that something they did—spin in a circle, bob their head—must have made the food appear in their cage. The lesson of those pigeons governs a lot of first-hand food. It's why we resort to playing Boz Scaggs when we fish, and it's why we visit the tree next to the Melody Tent parking lot every time we're within a five-mile radius.

I do understand that nothing I do makes the mushroom come up. But like the pigeons, I look for causal links. Maybe it's the rain or the humidity or the temperature or the time of year. And of course those are bona fide factors. They all play a role. It's just hard to suss out exactly what that role is and predict when the mushroom will appear.

So I bob my head and spin in a circle and drive by the tree as often as possible.

Primal Squeam

There is one more aspect of mushroom hunting we should discuss. It's true for wild food in general, and depending how you look at it, it's either a little embarrassing or a wonderful opportunity for personal growth.

When I was in college, I had a friend named Rachel. She grew up in a crunchy, earth-tone family, and she was forthright and capable and inattentive to niceties. We were eating lunch one day and a bug crawled out from behind a leaf in her salad. She didn't miss a beat. She picked the bug out, squished it in her fingers, and wiped its remains off with a napkin, talking all the while.

This made enough of an impression on me that I remember it clearly forty years later.

It made an impression because I wanted then, as I want now, to be more like Rachel. I want to pick the insect out of my food and continue eating, without giving it a second thought. What I actually do is pick the insect out of my food and continue eating, but hopefully without revealing that I'm grossed out.

There you have it. I don't like bugs in my food.

This is not the kind of person I want to be, but we get to choose the

HOW TO TELL IF A

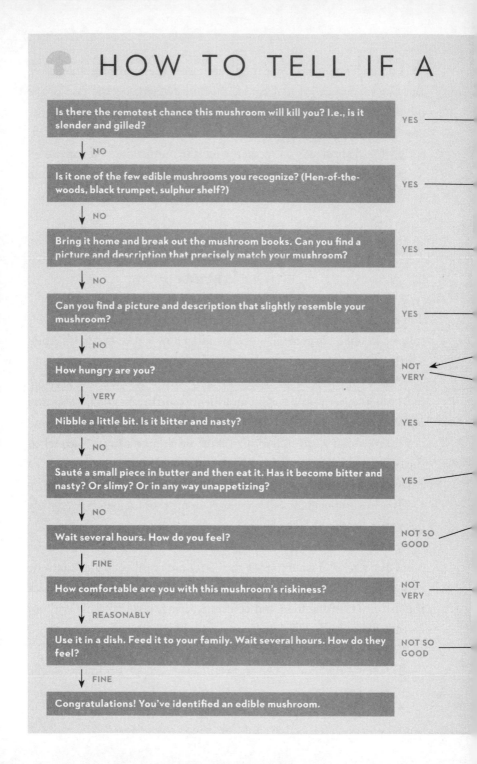

Is there the remotest chance this mushroom will kill you? I.e., is it slender and gilled? **YES** ——

↓ NO

Is it one of the few edible mushrooms you recognize? (Hen-of-the-woods, black trumpet, sulphur shelf?) **YES** ——

↓ NO

Bring it home and break out the mushroom books. Can you find a picture and description that precisely match your mushroom? **YES** ——

↓ NO

Can you find a picture and description that slightly resemble your mushroom? **YES** ——

↓ NO

How hungry are you? **NOT VERY**

↓ VERY

Nibble a little bit. Is it bitter and nasty? **YES** ——

↓ NO

Sauté a small piece in butter and then eat it. Has it become bitter and nasty? Or slimy? Or in any way unappetizing? **YES** ——

↓ NO

Wait several hours. How do you feel? **NOT SO GOOD**

↓ FINE

How comfortable are you with this mushroom's riskiness? **NOT VERY** ——

↓ REASONABLY

Use it in a dish. Feed it to your family. Wait several hours. How do they feel? **NOT SO GOOD** ——

↓ FINE

Congratulations! You've identified an edible mushroom.

MUSHROOM IS EDIBLE

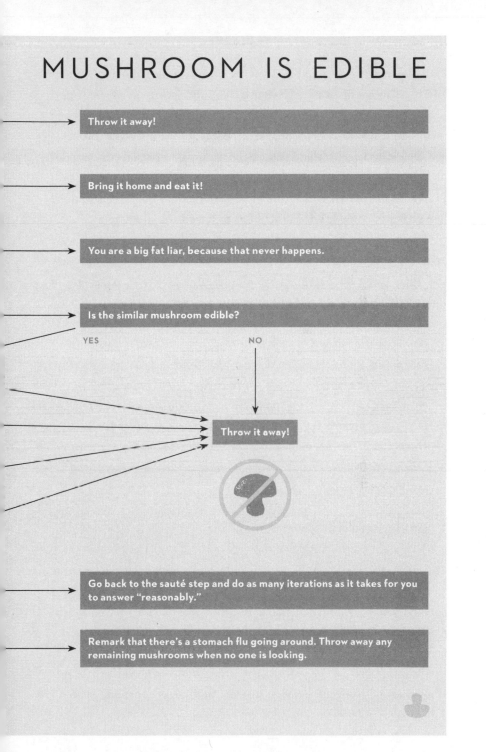

Throw it away!

Bring it home and eat it!

You are a big fat liar, because that never happens.

Is the similar mushroom edible?

YES   NO

Throw it away!

Go back to the sauté step and do as many iterations as it takes for you to answer "reasonably."

Remark that there's a stomach flu going around. Throw away any remaining mushrooms when no one is looking.

kind of person we want to be only within limits. I long ago decided that "Be Nice" was one of my rules for living, and I consciously became a nice person, and that works great! It brings me joy and fishing tips and makes all kinds of interactions with people go well. But I can decide and decide and decide that I want to be the kind of person who can just pick the bug out of her food and not care, but it doesn't work. The best I can do is *pretend* to be that kind of person. And it's not just that I don't like bugs in my food. I don't like bugs to have been in my food.

Psychologists have a name for this (psychologists seem to have a name for everything, something I will remember when we get a new cat). They call it *touch transference.* Here is how Helen M. Macbeth, in *Food Preferences and Taste: Continuity and Change,* describes it:

> *Americans are inclined to reject foods that have contacted a disgusting entity, such as a worm, cockroach or body waste product. The deep motivation in these rejections seems not to be fear of microbial infection, because the rejection is not substantially weakened if the disgusting contaminating agent is sterilized. The intuition here, even for educated Westerners, is that when a cockroach touches their mashed potatoes, even briefly with no visible residue, the potatoes have been "cockroached" and take on some cockroach properties.*

It's like homeopathy, but for disgusting.

To be fair, there's some evolutionary sense in this. Back before there was such a thing as microbiology, people who avoided germ incubators like feces and vomit and corpses lived to reproduce. In my defense, I will note that maggots are another bona fide indicator of "don't eat this!"—so I can be forgiven for being revolted by the worms floating out of my honey mushrooms.

Ordinary run-of-the-mill insects, though, aren't. Nevertheless, a mushroom with several holes in it is markedly less appealing than an intact specimen. I hate the idea that their little insect legs have crawled all over it and their little insect mandibles have ripped pieces out of it.

I recognize that it is unreasonable to object to wild creatures eating the wild fungi I want to eat—seems to me it's the insects who have the grievance here—and I know there are lots of cultures where they'd be thought of as extra protein. My repugnance is because I'm an "educated Westerner" with a learned disgust response.

I shouldn't be relying on my gut here. This is a problem for my head. There's nothing wrong with a plant that insects walked on or nibbled at, so just get over it! We've already discussed how unwilling brains are to override guts, but guts are also unwilling to be overridden; they don't like to do the bidding of rational thought.

Sometimes, though, you can wear them down with sheer persistence. I've been processing food we grow or forage for over a decade now, and dealing with those interlopers is a necessary part of the process. Don't get me wrong, I'm no Rachel! But I've slowly started to tolerate insects and even think of them as benign. Aphids gotta eat.

You don't have to go very far back in time to get to the point where most people had some role in procuring their own food, and insects in the lettuce was the least of their worries. Modernity insulates us from much harder hardships than that! Things like lack of plumbing and heating, brutal physical work, incurable infections and disease, and relentless, grinding poverty.

First-hand food is an exercise in selectively reintroducing the hardships of our choosing. Only, please, call it recreation. And it is way more fun when you don't have to do it.

It's also an antidote to what the modern food world throws at us. Because modernity was good for food, too, until it wasn't. Better ways to grow food, combined with better preservation and distribution, dramatically reduced starvation and malnourishment nearly everywhere in the world. But now, of course, we have the flip side, at least in developed countries: obesity and disease, primarily from eating foods very far removed from their plants and animals of origin.

Foraging moves us back. And of all the activities I've done, it has the lowest bar to entry. You can put this book down right now and head outside. I promise I won't be offended.

But somebody should warn the aphids.

CHAPTER 15

FORAGING'S LOW-HANGING FRUIT

Let's face it. A lot of forageable food is disappointing. But there are definitely enough bright spots to get you off the couch. Here are my top four:

FRUIT—It's in a fruit's evolutionary interest to be eaten (so its seeds spread through poop), and it's in a leaf's evolutionary interest not to be (so the plant survives), which is why fruits taste better than leaves. Wild berries, beach plums, and grapes are what's good in my neck of the woods, but I've heard tell of places where fig trees line the streets.

NUTS—On Cape Cod, the nut pickings are slim. There are acorns, of course, but you already know their shortcomings. We also have black walnuts, which are more useful than acorns but still aren't up there with almonds. Also, to crack them you have to run them over with the truck. Also, they turn your hands black. But if you live in a place where hazelnuts or pecans grow wild, you will have to fight me for them.

ANYTHING ONION—The alliums are a big happy family: onions, leeks, chives, garlic, and shallots. Wild versions grow almost everywhere, and

(continued)

they have the big advantage of being easy to identify; they smell like what they are. When in doubt, nibble.

A FEW MUSHROOMS—Do not eat any tall skinny gilled mushrooms unless you really know what you're doing. Even rank amateurs, though, can identify a few varieties that have no deadly look-alikes and are very tasty. Chanterelles, black trumpets, hen-of-the-woods, and chicken-of-the-woods (and yes, they're different) are all easy to ID. Porcinis aren't always obvious, but anything with pores instead of gills is likely to be safe and pretty much guaranteed not to be deadly. Although there is a false morel, it doesn't really look much like the real deal. Get a field guide and head out.

This list is necessarily limited by what I've figured out here in the Northeast, but one of the joys of foraging is serendipity. Wherever you are, look down. Look up. Smell. There's food all around us.

PART V

Turkeys

CHAPTER 16

POULTRY IN MOTION

You know how the grocery store puts M&M's and the *National Enquirer* right at the checkout? This is to maximize the chance that after you've made the carefully considered decision to buy green beans and *The Economist*, you have one last chance to be undone. Well, feed stores do it, too.

It was spring, a couple years into our chicken operation, and we were buying feed. And there, right at the checkout, were the M&M's of poultry: a couple of brooders full of chicks. On the left were white leghorns, but we were all chickened up and didn't need those.

On the right were turkeys. Standard bronze poults at $14.99 each.

Kevin and I had talked about turkeys. We'd even thought about getting them that spring, but we had a rule: one new species per year. Since we'd already gotten two hives of bees, turkeys were tentatively slated for the next year.

But there they were, cute little mottled brown poults about a week old. They looked very small and low-maintenance. We looked at each other, those birds and I.

Keeping chickens had taught us a lot about chickens, but the biggest lesson was that nothing about chickens is very hard. In some ways, turkeys had to be even easier. You keep them only five months, and you don't have to get them through a winter. Besides, how often had we forged ahead with nothing but the confidence that if people all over the world do something, we probably can, too?

People all over the world raise turkeys. We bought four.

A Building Trade

It's a good thing they started small, because they'd have to live in the wine box we brought them home in for at least a day or two. Turkeys, like chickens, spend their first few weeks in a brooder, and we'd lent the plastic box we'd used as a chicken brooder to a friend with chicks. Besides, we wanted something a little bigger, appropriate to a flock of birds that would grow pretty quickly. Our chicken brooder was the size of a laundry basket; this turkey brooder would be closer to the size of the washer you put the clothes in.

"Why don't you build it?" Kevin asked.

Why don't I build it?

Because Kevin is Vice President of Building Things. He's the one who's good with tools and materials. Structures are his magisterium. Under the Competent Spouse Doctrine, this is his job. I show up to remind him to wear safety glasses and to make sure he doesn't miss a spot.

By way of argument, Kevin invoked one of my all-time favorite *New Yorker* cartoons, which probably dates to the Clinton administration.

An executive is sitting behind a big desk in a fancy office, and there's a chimpanzee in a suit sitting across from him.

"You've had enough 'monkey see,' Edwards," the executive says. "We want some 'monkey do.'"

It was only fair. I'd learned at least enough to try a rudimentary project, and a brooder is the snickerdoodles of construction. Although I will add that I still don't understand why snickerdoodles are the standard-issue junior-high first baking project. Nobody even likes them, and brownies, which everyone likes, aren't any harder.

The first step of brooder construction was within my capabilities because it's just math, but Kevin gave me a hint: most building materials come in 4×8-foot sheets, so it makes sense to scale the brooder so you need only one. Because this was a small project, we figured we'd actually buy the materials rather than scrounge for them, so things like that were a consideration.

Can do! We needed a solid box with an open top, and if we made the floor 4 feet by 2 feet and the walls 2 feet high, we'd need exactly 32 square feet of . . . whatever. Maybe paneling, maybe light plywood—depends on what's cheapest at Home Depot. Then just the commensurate framing lumber, and we're done.

The cheapest choice that was likely to withstand rambunctious birds with sharp beaks and talons turned out to be the flimsiest grade of plywood. For framing, we got four 8-foot lengths of 2×3 lumber. We unloaded it in the garage, and Kevin made sure I knew where all the tools were.

"You're leaving?" I asked, trying to keep the plaintive out of my voice.

"I'll be in the house if you need me," he said, trying to keep the patronizing out of his.

"But you're not resigning your vice presidency, are you?" I couldn't be in charge of construction projects for all eternity.

"Monkey do, Edwards," he said. "Monkey do." He left me to it.

Well, okay then. I could do this.

I measured (twice) and cut (once) with a chop saw and a circular saw. I assembled with a hammer and nail guns, including the big hairy Porter Cable framing gun that Kevin nailed his fingers together with when we built the chicken coop. I am happy to report that I did not nail my fingers together. I even changed the design mid-construction, replacing one of the solid walls with hardware cloth so the birds could see out. Once or twice I needed Kevin to hold things in place as I hammered, sawed, and nailed, but I built the whole damn thing. He didn't have to remind me to wear safety glasses. And I didn't miss a spot.

When you were in preschool, did you have to make those potholders with the fabric loops that go on the little plastic loom? A teacher or camp counselor or babysitter gave you all the materials and showed you how to do it, and you spent a morning going over and under, over and under. When you were done (if you were me), you had a lumpy, misshapen potholder that nevertheless elicited compliments and praise. Nobody told you it was something any six-year-old could do.

That was the dynamic around here as I surveyed my finished brooder. The box was sturdy, the corners were square, there were no nails sticking out. I felt a little swell of pride at the sheer adequacy of it. Kevin didn't point out that as long as an adult was there to help with the power tools, although a six-year-old might not have been able to do it, a ten-year-old certainly could.

Funny thing, though. I found myself looking around for some other simple project. A planter? A bat box? Stilts? Still, I wouldn't be accepting Kevin's resignation anytime soon.

The turkeys were fine with it. We used the waterer from our last batch of chicks, and an old cast-iron pot for a feeder. We tossed in a bed of pine shavings, and our poults were home.

We figured they'd be fine in their brooder for a good month, but we had no idea what to do next. A month, though, gave us four whole weeks to figure it out; we've solved much harder problems in much less time.

Penmanship

Like chickens, baby turkeys stay cute for about eight seconds. And like chickens, they have a long, unattractive adolescence of scraggly feathers and ungainly lurches. But in other ways they're not like chickens. It wasn't long before they started chest-bumping and raising their tails, so they looked like ratty little imitations of picture-book turkeys. They were also growing. Fast.

Surprisingly, they didn't seem to be stupid. Turkey stupidity is the stuff of legend; they can supposedly drown by looking up in a rainstorm or simply not figuring out they should take their head out of their water dish. But ours seemed to have something going on in the brains department. Not the kind of thing that gets you into Yale early admission, but baseline street smarts.

From the day we brought them home, they were on the lookout for an escape route. Now, you could argue that escaping from a warm, predator-proof brooder into a cold, predator-rich world won't score you an 800 on the turkey SATs, but we thought this was a notable accomplishment for a bird a week old. Our chickens never showed that much initiative.

Since we expected the birds to be able to fly at least a little, and turkeys are big birds, we needed space. We also knew we couldn't make a big space predator-proof, but we wanted to at least give our predators something to think about. So we were aiming for a big, predator-resistant daytime space and a small, genuinely predator-proof house for the night.

The first step was finding a site. Our property is two acres, and we needed a space we could fence in relatively easily. If you've ever fenced anything in, you know that the issue with fences isn't fencing; it's fence posts. To keep fencing from falling over, fence posts have to be sturdy and sunk deep in the ground.

So ask yourself: what's sturdy and *already* sunk deep in the ground? Trees, of course! And we have many, many trees. So we went in search of a spot that was clear of brush, sheltered by leaf cover, and big enough to hold four turkeys. At least *I* was looking for a space big enough for four. Kevin was looking for a space big enough for eight, or even twelve.

"Twelve?" I asked.

"Turkeys are pretty easy so far," he said.

We found a spot just off the driveway. A couple of rhododendrons had to go—I figured we sacrificed them to the god of livestock—but it was otherwise ready to be turned into a pen.

Five cattle panels and two days later, we'd enclosed it. A couple of the spans between trees were almost exactly sixteen feet (the precise size of a cattle panel, as luck would have it), and we trimmed the other panels to fit. We attached the panels to the trees with big galvanized steel staples and, in a nod to predator resistance, ran a three-foot-high length of chicken wire around the bottom (it would also help contain the turkeys when they were small). And because I came out of my brooder-building experience brimming with confidence, I actually pulled my weight on this construction project.

The plan was for them to spend their days in the pen, but they needed a secure place to spend the night, off the ground and away from pesky nocturnal predators. For that, we were planning a tree house, but we had the fencing done before we even started building it. While we were figuring it out, the turkeys commuted. We put them in the pen during the day and returned them to their brooder in the garage at night.

They seemed to like the pen. They had room to run around, and there were some low tree branches they could reach. They scratched and explored, ate leaves and bugs, and seemed curious about their new environment. They also proved to be pretty scrappy.

As Kevin was taking tools in and out of the pen, he left the gate open and a couple of chickens wandered in. For a while, all the birds went about their business, apparently oblivious. But then the turkeys got the idea that this was *their* pen.

They went after the chickens in a posse, corralling them into a corner and pecking at them. The mature chickens were easily twice the size of the young turkeys at this point, but they also had the wisdom that presumably comes with age, and they knew no good comes of war. They fled.

In general, the turkeys turned out to be better company than we expected, and we spent a fair amount of time hanging out in the pen watching them watching us, which they do with a rather eerie, one-eyed, cocked-head stare. They would peck at our feet and roost on our arms if we sat down. One hopped on Kevin's shoulder and closely examined his ear. I will admit that, in retrospect, this doesn't exactly sound fascinating. But we'd never seen turkeys up close before, so every little thing was fresh and new.

I suspect they exceeded our expectations because our expectations were pretty low (that's a theme around here). We didn't think they'd be as charming as chickens, and they weren't, but we would find out a couple years down the road that they were *way* more charming than ducks. (We got a flock of Pekins once we got our poultry confidence up, and they made the turkeys seem like Cary Grant. They were messy, alarmist birds that waddled around the pen in a huddle. They were also absolutely delicious, but so challenging in the personality department that we never got them again.)

Turkeys, though, were climbing the poultry charts. Even though they were only a few weeks old, we already suspected they wouldn't be our last flock. We finished off their domain with a tree house to protect them from nighttime marauders, and we settled down for a summer of fattening them up for Thanksgiving.

Have you ever read about one of those well-intentioned philanthropic projects that goes wrong because the funders don't really understand the facts on the ground? Things like bringing computer kiosks to places where the electricity doesn't really work? We had this great pen, with its sturdy fence and secure tree house. But we made a tragic mistake in seriously underestimating our turkeys' ability to fly.

We expected some flight; that's why we gave them lots of space. But we'd also read that if you keep turkeys fenced in from the time they're very young, they'll respect fences. And for all I know, our turkeys did respect the fences. They may even have esteemed them. All I can tell you is that they flew over them.

Looking back, I can't even tell you what I expected without its sounding completely idiotic. A bird doesn't have to fly very well to get over a four-foot fence; even some of our more motivated chickens could do it. But I thought the turkeys would stay inside . . . why again? I have no idea. On what planet would a self-respecting bird not fly over a fence?

Not our planet, clearly. The turkeys did stay in the pen when we were in it, too; they seemed genuinely interested in the building of their tree house. When we left, though, they'd fly out and follow us. We talked about ways to keep them enclosed, but the fact that they were willing to follow us meant that it generally wasn't hard to get them back into the pen, so we let it slide.

We hadn't bargained on the Bedtime Wars. Anyone with children will understand.

Our plan was that the birds would roost in the tree house. Ha! The first night, their plan was to disappear just as evening set in. We looked in trees and bushes, and in the garage where the brooder had been. No turkeys.

We were worried, and I went out early the next morning to look for them. As soon as I walked out of the house, they came rushing out of the woods, half running, half flying, to see if I had anything to eat.

Bedtime Wars, round 1: turkeys.

We herded them back into the pen, where they stayed for most of the day. Periodically, one or two would fly over the fence, but once outside, they didn't seem to take advantage of the opportunities freedom afforded. Instead, they hung around by the fence, trying to get back in. Although every one of them was capable of flying out, not a single one managed to figure out how to reverse the process. I revised my assessment of turkey intelligence down a notch.

It was a revision I made with mixed feelings, since we seemed to be losing our effort to outsmart them.

The second night, as evening closed in, they showed no signs of wanting to go in the tree house. As the light began to fade, they started eyeing the treetops, but we didn't give them a chance. We put them bodily in the house. They protested mightily that it wasn't their bedtime yet. They begged for us to read them a story. They told us there were monsters under the bed. But we were ruthless, and we shut them in. And again the third night.

Bedtime Wars, round 2: humans.

The night after that, Kevin was bound and determined that the birds would go in the tree house of their own accord. As soon as the sun started to set, we put chairs outside the pen to watch what they'd do. (We took to calling this Turkey Theater.)

As it got darker, it became clear that their two nights in the tree house hadn't changed their habits. They started pacing the fence, looking up in the trees and making their weird croaking sound that's more like a seal's bark than a bird's peep. And then one made a break for it, flying right over the fence. Kevin corralled it and tossed it back in.

We waited. And then another one, or maybe the same one, flew up, over, and onto the woodpile. Kevin corralled it and tossed it back in. After the third breach of the fence, Kevin stood near the point they seemed to like to fly over and glared at them, willing them to go into the tree house. One of them flew right in his face.

Eventually we decided to resort to force again, and we put two of them in the tree house. Once we did, the other two followed.

Bedtime Wars, round 3: draw.

That first week, the turkeys refused to go in their tree house of their own volition, and there are only so many evenings you can spend trying to teach turkeys to roost in a tree house before you start to feel like there are better things to do with your time.

"That's it," said Kevin. "I'm putting up the net."

We went with a net not because that's the recommended material for keeping turkeys enclosed, but because we happened to have one. A big one: a hundred feet by twenty. Nets are used in clam farming, and ours was left over from our oyster farm's previous owner. We looped it around the edge of the pen's circumference, extending the four-foot-high fence's sides up to twelve feet.

That night, unlike the previous few nights, we were looking forward to Turkey Theater. We opened the wine and took our glasses out to the pen.

Sure enough, as the sun began to set, the turkeys started looking up in the trees. We watched them craning their necks, trying to find a trajectory that would take them up and over. We weren't sure whether they could see the top of the net; turkeys are reputed to have excellent eyesight, but a black net at dusk is tough to make out.

Eventually one of them made the attempt. He (or she—they were too young for us to tell) flew into the net and then tried to climb up it, flapping his wings madly. He only made about a foot of progress before he gave it up and half fell, half flew back down. There were two other forays, with similar results.

And then, miracle of miracles, one of the turkeys went into the tree house. Nobody else followed, so he came out again. I was sure he was going to ask for a glass of water. But after a while he just went back in. Then a second one joined him. Then the last two. They were all in, with no help from us. Hallelujah.

Bedtime Wars, round 4: humans.

We knew better than to declare victory. The turkeys could, in theory at least, fly over the net. "Stalag 17, it's not," said Kevin. But they'd need to first get on top of the tree house and then fly to the nearest point over the net from there. We could only hope that turkey stupidity was such that they never put that together. Most of the time they didn't, but occasionally they did.

Bedtime Wars, overall victor: turkeys.

Attempting to keep the turkeys contained cost me several *Green Acres* moments. Although I didn't watch much television as a child (this does not redound to my credit; my parents sneered until I turned it off), even I remember Eddie Albert and Eva Gabor leaving New York City and trying to make a go of it outside their natural habitat. Fortunately, in our version, both Kevin and I are Eddie Albert. Although we've never quite reached his level of haplessness, we certainly have his enthusiasm.

Most of the time.

As we bumbled through the turkey housing, I found my inner Eva asserting herself, reminding me of the charms of the city, where we didn't have to do battle with varmints, nobody tracked chicken poop into the house, and a turkey's ability to fly was irrelevant to the lifestyle.

I do appreciate fresh air. I do. But there were moments, in this project and others, when Times Square looked awfully good. When those moments happened, I tried to keep them to myself. My experience of the projects we were taking on was overwhelmingly positive, and I was confident that if I could just keep my chin up for a while, the enjoyment and satisfaction would invariably reassert themselves. Besides, it would be unfair to saddle Kevin with a wife who had Eva's longing for New York, but without the sexy Hungarian accent and the really nice boobs.

We came to a truce with the turkeys. They settled into a pattern where they would spend most of their time in the pen, roost in the trees either in the pen or close to it at night, and reliably return in the morning when I brought their breakfast. It wasn't optimal, but it was manageable. My inner Eva receded, and we turned our attention to getting the birds through to November.

All-Night Diners

With our first flock and our half-assed fence-and-netting setup, I left the feeder in the pen all the time, figuring that would keep the birds in close. Which it sort of did. But I noticed the level of the feed was going down awfully quickly.

I did the math.

We had four turkeys. When they were about two months old, they should have been eating three pounds of feed a week, give or take. That's twelve pounds total, so a fifty-pound bag should last a month, right? Okay, if it lasted three weeks I'd just figure they were big eaters. But when a bag was gone in seven days, I knew they were getting help.

I'd seen chipmunks going back and forth to the feeder, but it never occurred to me that the amount of food they could take was significant. Was it a zillion little chipmunks, taking a few pellets at a time, or one Chipzilla, making off with a pound at a go?

Unfortunately, it's impossible to chipmunk-proof a turkey feeder. If the turkeys can get the feed, so can the stripy little bastards, which you, too, will learn to hate if you try your hand at livestock. I had no immediate idea how to solve the problem, but I thought I'd get a better handle on it by putting out a trail camera—we call ours the VarmintCam—to find out just what was going on.

Oh, did I find out.

Picture after picture of chipmunks cavorting in the turkey feeder. They went in the little tray, they went up over the top, they picked up what fell on the ground.

They weren't the least little bit fazed by the presence of a turkey. While I am very susceptible to the appeal of cross-species harmony, there is no joy in pictures of chipmunks and turkeys breaking bread together, when I'm providing the bread.

Bold as brass, all day long, chipmunk after chipmunk. Or maybe it was the same two, over and over.

When night fell, there was a brief lull in the activity. And then, at 8:28 P.M., I learned the value of predator resistance. There was a raccoon. A big raccoon. Just sitting there stuffing his face. Or hers.

But wait, there's more! Two minutes later, the raccoon brought a friend. Two raccoons!

I scrolled through pictures on the camera. If anyone needs a photograph of two raccoons eating from a turkey feeder, I have 479 of them. Literally. The two raccoons partied all night long at our turkey feeder.

Okay, maybe not quite all night long. At around two A.M. they took a break. To let the opossums have a turn.

We learned the hard, stupid way that predator-resistant livestock housing is not a thing. Either you go the distance to predator-proof or just put out the welcome mat.

I took to putting the feeder out in the morning and taking it in at night. The chipmunks still got some, but I didn't feel quite as hostile toward them once I outwitted the bigger and thankfully nocturnal varmints—if taking the feeder indoors rises to the level of "outwitting."

Even without help, the turkeys started going through a lot of feed as they got bigger. And we started thinking about the event that had been looming since the day we brought them home.

The Trial Run

We came to Cape Cod with a little turkey experience, but only a little. It dated back to an afternoon early in our relationship—we'd probably been together a year or two—when Kevin, who was driving home to New York from Connecticut, called me from the side of the road.

"I just saw a wild turkey get hit on the Merritt Parkway," he said. "Do you want it?"

I paused, but not for long. "Yeah, I want it."

Another pause. "Do you know how to deal with a wild turkey?" I asked.

"No," answered Kevin, "but how hard can it be?"

I had about forty-five minutes to find out.

From the car, Kevin checked in with his friend Dave, who lives in the wilds of Vermont. Dave knew exactly what to do with the bird, but any instructions that begin with "drill a hole in a two-by-four" probably weren't going to work in a Manhattan apartment.

I began by calling my mother. She learned many rural lessons from Uncle Frank's farm, and I hoped poultry dressing was one of them. No dice. "Why don't you try the internet?" Mom suggested. Thanks, Mom.

That's what I did, and I got a crash course in field dressing wild turkeys. But a lot of the instructions were of the Dave variety; they naturally assumed you'd be doing this outdoors. We, however, would be doing it in the bathtub, so we'd have to adapt.

We were under the gun because we were meeting friends downtown for dinner at eight-thirty, and Kevin didn't pull up in front of the building until eight. He popped the trunk and took out the turkey.

If you've ever spent time in New York, you know that almost nothing raises New Yorkers' eyebrows. My father once saw a man in a gorilla suit, briefcase in hand, walk out of a midtown office building, and nobody paid the slightest attention. If, however, you take a twenty-four-pound wild turkey with a five-foot wingspan out of the trunk of a Saab, even jaded city dwellers stop and stare.

I'm not sure they were thinking, *Boy, are they lucky!* but that's how we felt.

I'd never seen a wild turkey up close, and I was surprised at its size and its beauty. Its body was a lustrous green-black, with a sweeping tail in rich dark orange and a bright red wattle. Its huge, powerful wings were tipped with brown-and-white-striped feathers. Turkeys are more often the butt of jokes than the objects of admiration, but this bird was spectacular.

The temperature outside was in the 30s, so we could bundle it into a trash bag and stash it in a corner of the building's courtyard while we met our friends. I warned the doorman that it was there. "Don't let anybody take it!" I said.

"Shouldn't be a problem," he deadpanned.

We just barely made it to dinner.

It happened that the friends we were meeting were all food people: a chef (Cathy), her partner (David), and a food writer (Alison). When we told them we had a wild turkey, Cathy's eyes lit up, and when dinner was over, she wanted to come uptown and help us deal with it.

By that time, it was eleven. Everyone but Kevin, who was driving, had had a fair bit of wine at dinner. I looked at David. "Are you in?" He nodded just a little bit wearily; he was used to Cathy's enthusiasm. And Alison? She was in, too. We piled into the Saab and headed back uptown.

We picked up the turkey from the courtyard and went up to our apartment. The first thing Kevin did was open another bottle of wine. "This has to continue to seem like a good idea," he said.

We put the turkey in the bathtub. We admired it and then strategized. One of the suggestions I'd gotten from my internet search was to dispense with the wings, which are hell to pluck and have very little meat. So we did. Next step was plucking, which made me very glad we had opted against the wings. Some of those feathers hung on for dear life, but we had six hands working on it. (Kevin and David figured three was the maximum a bathtub evisceration had room for; they stayed in the living room with the wine.) We stuffed the feathers in a garbage bag and moved on to the actual evisceration.

Plucking, at least, didn't require any skill; it was an exercise in brute force. To gut a bird, though, it really helps to know what you're doing. First step was to get the head off, a job most Manhattan apartments probably don't have the right tool for. The neck of a large wild turkey is about the size of my wrist, and most kitchen knives are no match for it. Neither are tin snips, it turned out. Finally Cathy, who cooks all day every day and has incredibly strong hands, held that bird by the neck and just wrenched the head off. We were all wildly impressed.

Since the incident of the turkey in the bathtub, I have gutted many birds. Even with experience, I sometimes find myself a little at sea trying to find exactly where the crop (a sac that acts as a holding tank for undigested food) attaches to the body cavity, or attempting to get everything out without perforating the bowel. If I had had to do it for the first time, a little tipsy, in the middle of the night, without help from a professional I'd probably still be there. Luckily, Cathy knew what she was doing, and the bird was done just before it stopped seeming like a good idea.

Last thing, though, Cathy told us the bird would improve if we could hang it in the cold air overnight. "Can you hang it out the window?" she asked. We lived on the sixth floor, and I could just imagine the field day headline writers would have with a pedestrian killed by a falling turkey carcass. So I opened the bathroom window and hung it from the shower instead. It scared the hell out of me when I got up to pee that night.

I roasted the bird in a clay pot, in a bid to keep it moist, and it was flavorful but squeaky-lean. It was reminiscent of one of the first free-range turkeys I'd bought some time in the early 1990s, which my mother nicknamed Turk LaLanne because it had zero body fat. But the soup from both those birds was top-notch.

I didn't know at the time that this bird would set the tone for so much of what we did afterward. It was the very first time we jumped into a project knowing absolutely nothing, the first time we bumbled through successfully, the first time we made a meal of something we'd gleaned from the world around us. And it proved we were well matched in this endeavor, because Kevin is the kind of man who brings home roadkill and I'm the kind of woman who wants it.

CHAPTER 17

PLUCK U.

The memory of plucking the turkey in the bathtub left an impression, and when we thought about doing that job times four, we started looking for ways to automate the process. There are lots of choices, and each and every one of them is on YouTube.

After watching hours of video and reading countless forums, Kevin decided that our course was clear. "Honey," he said, "I'm going to make us a chicken plucker. All I need is a washing machine and some chicken fingers."

Washing machine? I assumed that was for the motor. But the chicken fingers?

"No, not *those* chicken fingers," he said to me. "*These* chicken fingers." He held up his computer and showed me a site where you could buy a package of forty-eight black rubber finger-looking things for $29.99.

Although homemade chicken pluckers run the gamut, most are a variation on one theme: a rotating drum with black rubber protrusions.

Sometimes the fingers are on the inside and you put the chicken in the drum. Other times the fingers are on the outside and you hold the bird up to the fingers.

Kevin opted for the fingers-on-the-outside kind, because it seems like the chicken gets a pretty severe beating when it bounces around in the fingers-on-the-inside kind, and also because it looked like it might be a bit easier to build.

The chicken fingers, we bought with one click. For the washing machine, we went straight to Craigslist, which turned out to have washing machines galore. Kevin had only two criteria: it had to work, and it had to be cheap. Fortunately, a very nice guy in Orleans, a town about twenty miles up the Cape from us, was giving one away. When we picked it up, we told him what we were planning, and he seemed genuinely pleased that it would have a second useful life. Nobody likes to throw away working appliances, even if they are forty years old.

When we got it home and plugged it in, we were glad to find that it spun the way it was supposed to, even if it needed a little encouragement from a screwdriver to really get going. All we had to do was get the motor and drum out of its white metal housing, and we'd be well on our way.

This proved more difficult than I would have thought. It turned out that washing machine manufacturers make their housing pretty indestructible, or at least they did back in the seventies. So Kevin decided he had to take the radical step of tying one side of the housing to the garage and the other side to the Land Rover's front bumper and throwing it into reverse.

"Either the housing will open or the garage will fall down," he told me as he started backing up. I videoed it so that if he took down the garage, we would have the consolation of going viral.

Luckily, the housing opened.

We were left with a rotating drum and motor, still attached to the washing-machine console. It was forty-eight chicken fingers and an on/off switch away from being a chicken plucker.

The fingers were easy, if time-consuming. We just had to drill forty-eight ¾-inch holes and pop them in. The on/off switch was harder, because we discovered, too late, that the wiring diagram was on the inside of the housing, which we had already taken to the metal recycling pile at the dump.

We could wing it and see if we couldn't figure out which wires needed to be connected where to make a switch, but our winging-it policy, which is that we're always willing to do it, has a caveat about electricity and also plumbing. This is because of, respectively, electrocution and flooding. Sometimes you have to call in the professionals.

Nobody in the history of poultry management has plunked down cold hard cash to hire a bona fide electrician to work on a washing-machine chicken plucker, and we weren't about to be the first. Luckily, we could use the console as is. If we turned the knob to Spin, that's exactly what it did.

Besides, that way, if we got quail we could use Delicate.

All that remained was to mount the whole apparatus to something sturdy so it could do its thing while one of us held a bird against the spinning fingers. And that's when we had a design disagreement.

When you hold a bird against a spinning drum of rubber fingers, the feathers will fly everywhere. So in a perfect world, you mount the drum horizontally so the feathers fly downward, which will tend to make them stay contained, which will in turn make them easier to clean up. (If you believe that in a perfect world, you're not making a chicken plucker out of a washing machine, you don't know how to have a good time.) If the drum is vertical, the feathers will fly everywhere, and our neighbors had already borne with too many reminders of our livestock habit.

I nevertheless pushed for a vertical mount, because that's how the motor worked when it was still a washing machine. Turn a vertical drum horizontal, I figured, and all the stresses on all the parts would be wrong, and it might not work. Kevin thought that General Electric engineers, circa 1973, would never have designed so delicate and sensitive a machine. So we tried it horizontally.

A little trepidatiously, I turned the knob to Spin. It spun!

I took a step back to admire our work. Drum with fingers, mounted to two picnic table benches. Washing-machine console for the control. Blue tarp underneath to catch feathers. If any of you have gotten this far and are still doubting our hayseed credentials, I hope this makes up your mind. This was about as Dogpatch as it gets.

There was too much riding on our Thanksgiving dinner to wait until then to put the plucker through its paces. We needed a test run, which meant we needed someone who needed a chicken plucked.

Enter Sam.

Sam, who was sixteen at the time, is the son of my high school friend Ellen, who happens to live one town over. How we both ended up in the wilds of Cape Cod, a good 250 miles from our high school but a mere 5 miles from each other, is a mystery. It's probably not because Ellen and her husband, John, foresaw the day when we would need their son to bring his chickens over to test our plucker, but it sure worked out that way.

Sam had two hens—golden comets—that were reaching the end of their laying life, and he wanted to make room for his new flock. He volunteered them for our beta test.

This was going to be our first actual killing of livestock, and we did a lot of research to figure out the best way to do it. The time-tested old-fashioned way—cutting its head off—seemed like it might be hard to get right the first time around, and the prospect of doing it wrong and having a still-living chicken suffer the consequences was prohibitive.

After a broad survey of chicken-killing videos and forums, one method stood out as both the easiest and the most humane. You put the bird in an upside-down cone (people use traffic cones with the tip cut off), with its head out the bottom. One cut to the neck, just to sever the blood vessels, and the bird bleeds out. You have to be careful not to cut either trachea or esophagus.

A traffic cone would have been perfect, but we would have had to either buy or steal one. Instead, Kevin made a cone out of sheet metal, which we happened to have lying around, and attached it to a board. He mounted the board between two trees, and we had our Cone of Silence.

"Do you want to do this, or should I?" Kevin asked Sam.

Sam, whose willingness to try anything is one of the many reasons we like him, stepped up right away. He took one of his golden comets out of the box and put her in the cone. Her head hung out the bottom, and I handed Sam a knife that I had sharpened to the absolute best of my ability.

Kevin and Sam located the spot to cut, and Sam moved the feathers away and pulled the knife decisively across the bird's neck. He did it perfectly, and the chicken bled out. I was surprised at how simple, quick, and calm the process was.

Plucking was next, but it's easier if you first loosen the feathers by dunking the bird in hot water, and we had a pot heated to 160 degrees at the ready. Then it was time to put the plucker to the test.

Kevin had come to like using the console to start the plucker, probably because our particular model of washing machine was the kind his family had when he was a kid. He turned the knob to Spin.

We held our collective breath as Sam brought the bird in contact with the spinning fingers.

Miracle of miracles, the feathers flew! The thing worked.

Sam moved the bird around so first the legs, then the breast, and then the back came clean. He was having a little trouble getting into the crooks of the wings, but we finished those by hand. Everything was going smoothly until, midway through the second bird, the plucker shut down.

The motor was hot to the touch, and we thought it might have overheated, so we gave it some time to cool. After half an hour or so it did start back up, and we thought there was a good chance we could solve the overheating problem if we flipped the drum back to vertical. We called it a qualified success, and we started planning for the turkeys.

Dead Bird Walking

We still had a week before the turkeys' date with the Cone of Silence, and we were fattening them up with acorns and cracked corn. They of course weren't aware of their death sentence, but I sure was. I had been since the day we got them; it was the first time we'd raised animals we were planning to kill.

Up to that point, my killing experience was limited to fish, and I will admit to being uneasy. Kevin and I both take our livestock's lives very seriously, and a good death is integral to our idea of responsible stewardship. I wasn't looking forward to cutting the throat of a bird I'd raised from a poult, but part of the point of this whole first-hand food enterprise is stepping up to do the hard parts.

The day before what we'd taken to calling doomsday, we took their feed away. The point of this is to empty out the digestive tract. The less poop in the bird, the lower the probability of any kind of fecal contamination. The turkeys didn't like this one bit, and they were abnormally vocal and active the day before their death. There was a lot of barking in general, and a flock-wide sense of discontent. I was very sympathetic; take my food away and I'll show you discontent.

Doomsday dawned cold and cloudy, but with no rain in the forecast. As Kevin set up the plucker and the propane burner to heat the water, I went to pick up Sam, who had already proven his slaughter-day mettle and agreed to help us out. Our friend Amanda came, too, because she wanted to face the fact that birds have to die in order for us to have our Norman Rockwell Thanksgivings.

We also had a team from our local paper, the *Cape Cod Times*, coming. Our livestock venture, coupled with our willingness to eat roadkill, had made us small-town curiosities, and the paper was planning to cover the big event.

By ten-thirty that morning, we were ready to go. Kevin enlarged the cone to turkey size and the plucker, turned vertical, was standing by. The kitchen table was station evisceration, covered with newspaper and set up for gutting. The cooler was filled with 40 pounds of ice, ready for the finished birds.

The knives were very, very sharp.

Kevin did the first one, one of the three toms. Plucked him out of the pen, turned him upside down, and put him in the cone. The turkey's head came through the bottom, and Kevin cleared the neck feathers. "Thank you," he said, and slit his throat. And that was it. In moments, it was over.

The blood poured from the bird's neck, but as with the chickens, there was no struggle. The bird appeared to lose consciousness almost immediately, which would make sense, since no blood was reaching his brain. After about half a minute, the legs kicked a bit. We'd read that this happens as the heart stops.

And then it was my turn.

If I had been watching a movie where someone slaughters a turkey, this is the point at which I would look away. But there's a scene in the movie *Cold Mountain* that sticks in my mind.

Jude Law, having deserted from the Confederate Army, is on the run. In the forest, he finds a woman who keeps goats. She's not afraid of him, and she talks to him about the merits of goats as one of the animals has its head in her lap. She strokes the goat gently, and then, without interrupting the conversation, calmly cuts its throat.

That, I have always thought, is how to kill an animal.

Death looms large for us humans, but what makes it significant is the awareness that there is such a thing as life and that it is ending. I am willing to kill an animal for food in part because it doesn't have that awareness, and the harm I do is limited to the pain and distress I inflict in the process. The turkey or duck or pig doesn't know its life is ending.

The knife stroke that takes my bird's life is a fraction of a second's worth of pain. A bullet or a bolt gun, used on a larger animal, should kill it or render it unconscious instantly. Of course, the process doesn't always go as planned, and we have, over the years, made mistakes. Not many, but each one is gut-wrenching.

For that first turkey, and for every animal I've killed since, the most important part has been setting my emotions about killing aside so that I could focus on the process (maybe that's why they call it *execution*). It's like any other physical skill, but with higher stakes than, say, hammering the shingles on the chicken coop roof. You have to do it well; it has to be quick and decisive, deep enough to sever the blood vessels but not so deep as to hit esophagus or trachea.

Kevin handed me the knife and took the second turkey out of the pen. It was the one hen of the flock, and he tucked her under his arm and talked to her as he walked over to the cone and threaded her head through.

I kept thinking about what Atul Gawande wrote about his surgical training—how difficult it was for him to make that first cut into that first patient to insert a central line, but also how necessary it was that people learn to do these things, because that's the only way we can continue to do them. I was very glad this was a turkey and not a human.

Even so, that one knife stroke was the single most difficult thing I'd done since we started this enterprise. And it was over in an instant. It surprised me that the turkey didn't even flinch, and it was with relief that I saw the blood come pouring out, just as it was supposed to.

On the one hand, I feel a little silly making such a big deal out of something that humans have been taking in stride for millennia. On the other, I never want to be cavalier or careless about taking an animal's life.

We took it seriously, and we did it well. All four birds went smoothly, and within fifteen minutes we had four carcasses lined up on the truck tailgate. I felt my gut unclench. From here on out, I could make as many mistakes as I wanted.

Deep breath. And we move on to plucking.

First we scalded the birds to loosen the feathers. We'd heated the water in our only vessel big enough to hold a twenty-odd-pound bird: a galvanized steel garbage can. (We put it in our outdoor shower in the hopes both that it would be shielded from the wind and that it would go unnoticed by the media, but the photographer borrowed our ladder just to get a good picture of a turkey being dipped in a steaming garbage can.)

Once the bird was scalded, its feathers came out surprisingly easily. We pulled out the biggest tail and wing feathers by hand, and then Kevin fired up the plucker.

When we turned the machine from horizontal to vertical, it definitely ran better, but we were still unsure about its long-term viability. It started right up when Kevin turned it on, but we had a long way to go.

He held the first bird against the rubber plucker fingers, and again the feathers flew. We'd positioned it in front of the woodshed in the hopes of sparing our neighbors, and most of the feathers went where they were supposed to. Kevin had done a turkey and a half when I smelled smoke.

I looked down at the motor. Sure enough, it was smoking. And then I looked again. There was an actual genuine flame licking out of the back.

"Um . . . honey?" I said.

"Yeah?" Kevin said, adjusting the turkey so the plucker could reach its legs.

"The plucker's on fire."

My husband has many fine qualities. He is smart and funny, fearless and true. He is kind and curious and well informed. He always does the right thing. But at this point in the story, I feel obligated to mention that safety consciousness doesn't top his list of personal assets.

When I told him the machine he was using was in the process of going up in flames, what he said was . . . "Naaaah."

"Um . . . yeah." That was Amanda. She saw the flame, too.

Kevin didn't even look. HE DIDN'T EVEN LOOK.

"It's just a little smoke," he said.

And then the machine shut down.

"I think it's had the bananas," I said. This is a phrase I get from my mother, and it means kaput. Neither she nor I know where it comes from, but it is an excellent phrase that you will also want to use when your chicken plucker catches fire.

At that point, Kevin did look. But he didn't agree with my assessment.

"No, the spin cycle's just over," he said.

But it wasn't. It had definitely had the bananas. It did not go back on again. It was an ex–chicken plucker.

I braced myself for the rigors of hand-plucking, but I learned that if you're dealing with a freshly killed bird that's been scalded, it's not hard at all.

We also learned why almost all commercially raised turkeys are white. Dark feathers can leave pigment behind, unattractive little black dots marring the whitish-yellow skin. When we compared the machine-plucked to the hand-plucked birds, it was clear that machine plucking was more likely to leave black spots behind. Not that this should discourage you from making your own Rube Goldberg plucker! It's part of the fun of raising poultry. The spots are harmless, and you really can't see them once the bird is roasted.

Once they were plucked, we had to get their heads off. Cathy wasn't there to help, but we own much bigger knives than we did in New York and Kevin macheted them off.

At this point I will warn you, because I sure wish somebody had warned me, that birds that have been really and truly dead for quite some time can still move and it is beyond creepy. I was carrying one into the house—I had it by the neck—and it writhed in my hand. I almost dropped it on the driveway. And then when we brought another one in and put it on the table, I swear its heart beat. Or maybe it was a contraction of some other muscle in the vicinity of the heart, but we all saw it and it sure looked like *lub-dub, lub-dub.*

On second thought, warning you probably won't help. No amount of understanding that muscle spasms can happen after death (even in humans) will make it any less disconcerting.

So there I was, standing in my kitchen looking at four turkey carcasses that I was supposed to gut, when my only previous experience was watching someone else do it in the bathtub, in the middle of the night, kinda drunk. Then there was the fact that although the carcasses looked like they were holding still, I was a little afraid they'd get up and do the Charleston. And, in case you've forgotten in this onslaught of fascinating detail, the media was in attendance. This was being filmed.

I'd watched a lot of videos. I'd studied the anatomy. But there's a limit to the utility of book learning in a situation like this. As is true of so many of the things we do around here, the only way to learn to do it is to actually do it.

I did it, but it took me an unconscionably long time. Just doing the first step, which is removing the crop, took a good ten minutes. It sounds so simple, but the outside of the crop is attached to the inside of the skin, and the crop's outside looks exactly like the skin's inside and it's hard to find the interface.

Things improved after I managed that, and then I severed the trachea and esophagus as far down as I could reach. Then you have to go to the other end and cut an opening into the body cavity, cutting around the bowel at the anus. If you manage to do that without perforating anything important, you're almost there. You just reach your hand up into the bird and pull all its innards out the bottom.

A lot of people, including Kevin, find it icky, but I think it's satisfying to pull out the entire insides of a still-warm bird. That's the point where it finishes its transition to meat, and it goes into an ice bath to cool. This means my job is done. In a little less than an hour, it had gone from being a gobbling, pecking, living, breathing turkey to being a fourteen-pound oven-ready roaster—a remarkable transformation.

It was also, for me, a seminal and moving experience.

Over the years, we've had several turkey flocks, as well as ducks, meat chickens, and pigs, and we've never done slaughter day alone. We've always been joined by friends, or sometimes strangers, who feel that if they're going to eat meat, they need to know what it feels like to kill an animal.

This has surprised me. I didn't think people wanted to meet the livestock that becomes their dinner—I had to go back only a few years to a me who definitely didn't. I came around to it slowly, by wading deeper and deeper into projects involving plants and animals, and having my food sensibilities recalibrate as I went along. Of course I always knew that food came from plants and animals, but by dealing with the actual plants, and the actual animals, I internalized it in a way that I never would have, had we stayed in Manhattan.

Along the way, I learned a few things. First, and most disconcerting, is that killing gets easier, at least for me. None of the subsequent birds I've killed were as difficult as that first turkey, and I can see how constant repetition might harden me. Luckily, I don't get that constant repetition, but my heart goes out to the people who have the unenviable kill-floor jobs at slaughterhouses. If I ever pick up a knife and find myself unconcerned about taking a life, I will put that knife down and figure out what's gone wrong.

I also learned that I could like the animal and also like the meat. The first time we put a bird that we'd raised on the table, I wasn't sure how I'd feel about it. This is Drumstick, the alpha male of our first flock, roasted to a turn and served with gravy. But the overwhelming feeling turned out to be pride. We had given that bird an excellent life and a quick, calm death; it felt absolutely right to eat him. That's why he existed. I worried all over again when we had pigs, which are much more likable than turkeys, but the feeling was the same.

Kevin learned that the best, easiest DIY chicken plucker is rubber fingers on a PVC pipe that you attach to an electric drill to rotate. But we both have fond memories of the washing machine.

Despite the glaring problems with our food system, I'm not nostalgic for the times when everyone kept livestock in the backyard because that was the only way to survive. Give me abundance over scarcity, any day. I have nevertheless found value in doing the things that ordinary people have done for the entire expanse of human history, in the often-hardscrabble effort to feed themselves.

It's a testament to how far we've come as a civilization that a middle-aged couple raising and slaughtering four turkeys makes the front page of the local paper. There was a giant picture of us with one of the birds, and the headline LIVING OFF THE LAND.

This led to months of awkward encounters when we were recognized at the local supermarket. Strangers would look at us, cock their heads with that "aren't you the people . . ." look, and then crane their necks to try and see what was in our shopping basket.

"Paper towels," Kevin would say. "We're really just here for the paper towels."

CHAPTER 18

PICK YOUR POULTRY

⋙ WHICH MEAT BIRD IS RIGHT FOR YOU? ⋘

Gardens are easy. Laying hens aren't that much harder. But getting livestock you're going to kill is a big step—which is exactly why I recommend it.

But which? Here are the three I can weigh in on. (If you're thinking about geese or quail, you're out of luck.)

DUCKS

Our Pekin ducks were undoubtedly the tastiest birds we raised. But we will also never raise them again. They are smelly, messy, and xenophobic. Remember the scene in *Take the Money and Run* where Woody Allen is chained to his fellow escapees and they all have to shuffle around really close together? That's what ducks do.

They are also slow learners. You walk into the pen and they flee as a group to the farthest corner of the pen, despite the fact that you've entered the pen countless times before and it's always to bring them food. This went on for the entire eight weeks of their existence.

You slaughter ducks the same way you slaughter chickens, but plucking a bird that has the kind of feathering built for swimming is a pain. You probably have to resort to waxing off the underlayer of feathers. We did, at least. Plucking ducks sucks.

But they are damn delicious, and other people with other breeds, or even sometimes the same breed, have had better experiences than we did.

MEAT CHICKENS

Big Chicken, in its effort to produce ever more chickens for ever less money, has bred meat birds to have giant breasts and absolutely no gumption. There's just no way around it: they're a little bit disgusting.

They're fine when they're chicks, and for the first few weeks. But as they grow, which they do alarmingly quickly, they get less and less inclined to move around. They nestle on the ground, too often in their own poop, and their chest feathers sometimes wear off. They have nothing that resembles a personality.

That said, they produce a lot of meat very quickly—which is, after all, their reason for being. You can go from chick to slaughter inside six weeks. If we tackle meat chickens again, though, we'll go with a slower-growing bird (there are many choices) that still retains some chickenness.

TURKEYS

Turkeys take much longer than ducks—about five months—and if you've gotten this far, you know about the housing issues. But they're our hands-down favorites.

If you had told me when we had that first flock that we'd pick turkeys for their personality, I'd have laughed you out of the barnyard. But we grew much fonder of them after we'd been exposed to their competitors.

I also like turkeys because you get a lot of meals for the life taken (that's also a reason I like pigs, but I figure they're not on most people's radar). If people eat smaller pieces of larger animals, fewer animals have to die for our meat habit. This is why I don't eat quail.

I would be remiss if I didn't mention that our homegrown turkeys have been delicious. They have an excellent balance of fat and flavor, and they have been a hit at every Thanksgiving table.

PART VI

Hunting

CHAPTER 19

WHEN A GATHERER HUNTS

I am going to tell you about hunting, but first I am going to tell you about Kevin.

You already know he's a risk-taker. He is undaunted by thin ice, either literal or figurative. He plays fast and loose with power tools. For a living, he traded commodities, one of the few jobs where you can go to work and lose money. A lot of money. All your money, even.

It was back in his trading days that he earned his nickname: Crash. He got it not for his trading but for his skiing. He was known for spectacular falls that left hundred-yard trails of ski equipment that his friends had to follow, like bread crumbs, to find him in the snowbank. He has since solidified his reputation with motorcycles, cars, boats, surfboards, bicycles, and even a golf cart, which he drove, full throttle, over what he took for a hill but was actually the upper lip of a sand trap.

His full-throttle tendencies were apparent to me early on; we'd been dating only a few weeks when he told me he loved me. I marveled at his willingness to lay his cards on the table and make himself vulnerable, particularly since most men I dated seemed to make protecting themselves a high priority.

"It's the only way I know to get what I want," he said.

Horatio Lord Nelson, hero of the British navy and legendary victor at the Battle of Trafalgar, is said to have summed up his military strategy simply: "Never mind maneuvers. Go straight at 'em." Those tactics lost him an arm and an eye, but won him fame, fortune, and his perch on a column in Trafalgar Square. Nelson got what he wanted. And so did Kevin.

And so did I. Risk-taking is a breed of courage, and courage is just one of the old-fashioned virtues my husband came with. But it gives you pause, if your husband's nickname is Crash, when he wants to bring guns into the house.

To understand how this went down, you need a little history. I come from a middle-class Jewish suburban family, and nothing about my background prepared me for guns. I grew up with the Weavers, *The New York Review of Books*, and an aboveground pool. Firearms were alien to the lifestyle. "Guns don't kill people," the sentiment seemed to be. "Goyim kill people."

Whether I come by it culturally or personally, I hate guns. They scare me. So shortly after we moved in together, when Kevin wanted to use the front closet to store his two shotguns—a 12-gauge Browning Citori and a Remington 410—oh boy did I balk. Not only did it mean guns in the house, but it was also, strictly speaking, a crime.

New York City has some of the strictest gun laws in the country, and to get a permit for a rifle or shotgun, you had to go through a process that involved a background check, a personal interview, and the forking over of a hefty fee. Since Kevin had no intention of actually using the guns—he had previously used them for trap and skeet—he also had no intention of alerting the authorities to their presence in our apartment.

When he told me about this plan, I had to resort to one of my Marital Management Tools: the Reverse Terminator.

If you've seen *The Terminator*, you know what I'm talking about. There's a scene where the janitor knocks on the door of Arnold Schwarzenegger's fetid flophouse room and asks him if he's got a dead cat in there. Viewers watch Arnold's alien "brain" cycle through a host of reasonable responses: "Yes," "No," "Please come back later," even "Go away." The one he picks is: "Fuck you, asshole."

When faced with the possibility of moving guns into the house, I went through the same exercise in reverse. "No firearms in the house!" "That is a crime!" "No one whose nickname is Crash gets a gun!" are all options, but I settled on an anemic "Honey, I'm not sure I'm comfortable with that." Because my husband is not an idiot, he knows perfectly well that what I mean is, "No firearms in the house!"

He also knows that I am Reverse Terminating, something he can do, too. I watch him mentally scroll through options I prefer not to dwell on before he arrives at, "I promise there will be no ammunition. Without ammunition, they're just tubes."

I like to think I'm a reasonable person, and that certainly seemed like a reasonable argument. But we were in brain versus gut territory again, and my gut was hell-bent on no firearms in the house. But it seemed to me that I would have a hard time defending the idea that I was a reasonable person if I objected to tubes.

We put them way in the back of the top shelf.

If this was indeed a crime, I can only hope that the statute of limitations has expired, or that the New York City authorities have bigger fish to fry.

When we moved to Cape Cod, the guns went way in the back of the top shelf of a different closet, where they stayed until I decided that if I was serious about eating from the landscape around us, I had to think about hunting.

It took me some time and even some effort just to think about it. When we embarked on our first-hand food-a-day enterprise, the benign projects were top of mind. Gardening, laying hens, foraging, puppies, rainbows. It was nature without the teeth and the claws.

After we'd spent a few years on the Cape, the tooth and claw were coming home to me. Partly it was because I killed a few things, starting with fish but graduating to livestock. But I also found that living in the sticks was changing my relationship with the creatures I share the planet with. You realize, after a while, that your furry friends are all out to get you.

When you live in the city, there are three major categories of animals: the kind you see in the zoo, the kind that makes too much noise in the apartment next door, and cockroaches. There are also rats, pigeons, and those little eely things you find in the bathtub, but I include those in the cockroach category.

Out in the sticks, it's us versus them, and the categories are simpler: prey and not-prey.

Take rabbits. We have them. And at first I thought they were not-prey. Sure, they're edible, but they're cute and furry and I enjoyed seeing them hopping around the property. Until they hopped into the cabbages, at which point they suddenly became prey.

Okay, they were still cute and furry, and my relationship with them—and all the wild creatures we live among—didn't turn on a dime. It was a slow and somewhat unsettling process to go from seeing them as friends to seeing them as enemies, because it wasn't about the rabbits at all. It was about me. At what point did I go from live-and-let-live cute-animal lover to stone-cold killer?

But a serious effort to glean dinner from the landscape around you, which our project had become, pits you against animals that you have the luxury of not wanting to kill when someone else is getting your food for you. I began to see those guns at the back of the closet in a different light.

The problem was, we couldn't use them. There are laws about where you can discharge guns, and a good thing, too. You can't use a firearm within five hundred feet of a dwelling, and we had neighbors close enough to rule out the 410. But we'd also acquired a .22 air rifle, which isn't technically a firearm, and that did the job on our cabbage-loving rabbit. Well, actually, Kevin did the job using that particular tool and handed the carcass off to me. I skinned it, cleaned it, and braised it in beer with white beans and carrots.

Prey gets to be prey either because you want to eat it or it wants to eat what you want to eat. Even so, no matter how menacing it is to my livestock, I apply the same rule to backyard pests as I did to fish: I will not kill anything I'm not willing to eat. And I have the raccoon sauerbraten recipe to prove it.

In order to be not-prey, you have to taste bad (and I have to know it *before* I turn you into sauerbraten). Or maybe be very small. Although the woodpeckers threaten our way of life with their insistence on drilling holes in our house, they can go about their little peckerhead business in perfect safety.

Deer are definitely prey. They are large and they are delicious. They also check another prey box: there are way too many of them. Although Cape Cod is not one of the areas positively overrun with deer, even here they are in no danger of extinction. Eating overpopulated animals seems to me to be about the most responsible way to eat meat.

Lots of people, of course, believe that eating meat can't be responsible because it's unethical to take an animal's life. Although I don't share that position (obviously), I am sympathetic to it. I admire a principled position, even when it's not my principle.

But keeping humans fed is an animal-killing enterprise. Although vegetarianism keeps the evidence off the dinner table, the animals we don't see, killed by machinery, chemicals, and habitat destruction, are just as dead. I can't find reliable data on how many rats get poisoned each year to keep them out of the grain stores, but spare a thought for them when you reach for a dinner roll. Eating small pieces of large, carefully chosen animals might be a more humane choice than eating only plants. We'd need the rat numbers to figure it out.

For me, the question isn't whether we should kill animals or not kill animals, it's how to minimize suffering. I opt out of most conventionally raised meat because I don't like how the animals in our system are treated; my priority is to try to make sure the animals I eat have a decent life and a humane death. The decency of a wild animal's life is probably debatable, and some are undoubtedly better than others, but at least it's not a cage. As their death options go, a clean shot by a hunter is probably one of the better options. Sure beats starvation.

My qualms about killing animals for food aren't ethical, they're visceral, born of squeamishness and cowardice, and I had to face them down when we killed our turkeys. But going out in the world and pointing a loaded gun at a wild animal was a whole new level. The live-and-let-live cute-animal lover in me would not be completely quelled. I had spent an entire lifetime rooting for the gazelles on *Wild Kingdom* because I couldn't bear to watch the lions win. I was still, at heart, a gatherer.

But this entire exercise was supposed to be about expanding horizons and pushing comfort zones. I was convinced that eating overpopulated (or at least unthreatened) animals was responsible and planet-friendly, and that the only reason I didn't want to hunt was because I was a sniveling coward. So for my forty-seventh birthday I got a 20-gauge shotgun. Also a crew cut, but that is neither here nor there.

Then I set out to learn how to use it.

Old Dog, Meet New Trick

If I had my childhood to do all over again, I'd make some changes. For starters, I'd read more. My mother says she was sorely tempted to raise us in a way that was downright Dickensian. She wanted to lock us up with books with the daily admonishment that "These are the memorizing years!" I'm sure that, had she actually done it, it would not have gone over well with me and my brothers, but I'd definitely know more Roman history.

I would also have made it a point to learn to golf, to ski, and to speak French. And to handle firearms.

My first foray into learning that particular skill came forty years late, in the form of Hunter Safety class. Massachusetts law requires that before you are permitted to buy a gun or possess one on public property, you must have a firearms permit. To get the permit, you have to take the class.

It runs some eighteen hours over several days, and the instructors are volunteers. It covers all the topics you'd expect—firearm safety, gun laws, hunting basics—as well as some you wouldn't. I enjoyed the module on orienteering, which had us using a compass to navigate around a graveyard.

Over and over, in every module, every instructor emphasized the single most important rule of guns: always point the muzzle in a safe direction.

As you know, I'm rather fond of straightforward rules, and you wouldn't think that would be so hard, would you? Is that really something you can't learn to do as an adult? I wouldn't have thought so, until I actually tried to do it and also met Andre.

When we first met him, Andre was somewhere in the neighborhood of eighty years old, but unless you were pretty tough, he could probably still take you. Kevin called him the Jack Palance of Cape Cod. He was doing a lot of the things we were, with energy to spare. He fished and shellfished and gardened. He and his wife, Elsa, have seven acres, a few sheep, and a legendary asparagus patch. And he hunted.

Andre's father must have had a Dickensian streak, because he gave

Andre a wooden gun when he was eight years old and told him he couldn't have a real one until he proved that he could handle the wooden one safely.

That took four—count 'em, four!—years. Four years at an age when you're good at learning stuff! Four years, mostly to learn one rule: always point the muzzle in a safe direction.

The tricky thing about that rule, though, is that you have to internalize it. You have to commit it to whatever part of the brain is responsible for automatic stuff. Otherwise, you have to actively think about it CONSTANTLY.

Point the muzzle in a safe direction.
Point the muzzle in a safe direction.
Point the muzzle in a safe direction.
Are we out of peanut butter?

And, just like that, the muzzle is pointed in an unsafe direction. Meaning at someone.

When I went out with Kevin and Andre to shoot an actual gun for the very first time, I was less concerned with hitting the target than I was with always pointing the muzzle in a safe direction. If you do that, you're likely to achieve the single most important goal of hunting: don't shoot anyone.

That's necessary for a good hunt, but it's really not sufficient. At some point, you have to start thinking about hitting your target, too.

I wasn't sure what my real-life target was going to be. Yes, I wanted a deer, but I wanted to try birds as well; there are robust populations of both upland birds and waterfowl on Cape Cod. And this is where a distinction that's something of a rural litmus test comes into play. I am ashamed to admit it, but before I moved to the sticks, I didn't know the difference between a rifle and a shotgun. Let me show off my shiny new knowledge by explaining it to you.

The inside of the barrel of a shotgun is smooth, and the ordinary projectile is a pack of little metal balls (shot) that disperse as they leave the muzzle of the gun.

The inside of the barrel of a rifle is, as the name implies, rifled. That is, it has grooves that run in a spiral down its length. They give spin to the projectile, which is a bullet, and the spin imparts both speed and accuracy.

For reasons that have more to do with gun laws than ballistic science, a shotgun with a rifled barrel is still a shotgun. The walls of the barrel are thinner than that of a rifle, and a shotgun fitted with a rifled barrel doesn't have the long-distance range that rifles have.

If you're hunting birds, you use a shotgun, and you have the challenge of shooting a flying target. If you're hunting deer, you use a rifle or a shotgun with a rifled barrel. The gun and ideally the target are both stationary. (In Massachusetts, as in some other densely populated states, rifles are prohibited in hunting.)

Despite the moving-target problem, birds seemed like a lower hurdle than deer because there are so many of them and they're so easy to find; that's what Kevin and I were practicing for with Andre. He had a target thrower—a catapult that throws clay disks that mimic birds in flight—and we set it up in the back of our pickup and took it to the range.

Kevin learned to shoot when he was in his twenties, and he's good. He brought his 12-gauge, and he was up first. "Pull!" (This is what you say when you're ready for the target thrower to throw the target, just like on those British period pieces on TV.)

Andre pulled, and the clay disk came flying. Kevin hit it, apparently effortlessly. In fact, he hit nine out of the first ten, and that's after not having held a gun for god knows how long.

"You're a good shot," Andre said, clearly impressed. (It's very satisfying to impress Andre.)

Then it was my turn.

Point the muzzle in a safe direction.
Point the muzzle in a safe direction.

"Pull!"

I hit about three or four of the first ten, and they were the easy ones—thrown from behind me and going away from me. I struggled more when I moved to the side of the range and had to shoot targets that were going across my field of view. Andre was not impressed.

I, however, considered it a triumph because I kept the muzzle pointed in a safe direction.

Andre helped me figure out that I was making a couple of fundamental mistakes. For starters, I was tracking the target with the gun so the muzzle was always a little below it. What you're supposed to do is cover the target with the muzzle. If you can see the clay (or the bird) hovering over the bead on your gun, you're going to miss it low. Cover the target and move with it as you shoot.

My biggest problem, though, was that I wasn't mounting the gun to the same spot on my shoulder and cheek every time. The essence of marksmanship is consistency; if you don't put the gun in the same place, you won't get the same shot. Mounting a gun is just another of those physical skills that you ought to learn when you're a kid, and the only way to get it right is to make your body learn it by doing it the same way over and over and over.

One of the reasons I was having particular trouble with the pesky "same way" problem is because I happen to have a long neck. When you shoot, the butt of the gun rests against your shoulder, and your cheek rests on the top of the stock (the comb, it's called), and those of us over-endowed in the neck department have to do considerable scrunching to get both cheek and shoulder to where they need to be. (There are solutions for this, and once I put a pad on the stock I did better.)

But the other reason is that it was just plain hard to make a forty-something-year-old body internalize a new skill. After my lesson with

Andre, I practiced a lot. I walked around with the gun (unloaded), bringing it to my shoulder over and over. All the while remembering to *point the muzzle in a safe direction*. I got better, but I can't say I got good.

It turned out not to matter much because I hated bird hunting.

I hated it because neither kind of bird—upland game and waterfowl—turned out to be a viable choice. For the upland birds, you really need a dog, and we don't have one. The subset of waterfowl that we have on Cape Cod are, with few exceptions, the kinds of seabirds that taste like low tide. The eider I shot was definitely not an exception, and the best part about that hunt was that I got to shout, "Eider down!"

In case it's not clear by now, I am in this for the food. So I wrapped up my bird-hunting career pretty quickly and turned my attention to deer.

CHAPTER 20

DEER ME

Practice-wise, it was back to the drawing board. I had to set aside my shotgun training, such as it was, and switch to rifles—or in my case, the rifled barrel that my 20-gauge shotgun came with. Just unscrew the shotgun barrel, screw in the rifled barrel, and voilà! you're a deer hunter.

"You're going to need some slugs," Kevin told me as we were taking inventory of our deer-hunting paraphernalia.

Slugs? I know you can go hunting with dogs, and they flush the birds for you. You can go hunting with falcons and they will actually kill your prey and bring it back to you. But slugs?

No, not *those* kinds of slugs. The kind of slugs that are like bullets, only housed in a shell that fits it to a shotgun rather than a rifle. If it had been my call, I would have called them something else to avoid confusion, but nobody asked me.

Kevin also said it would make sense to wear the kind of clothing we'd wear hunting, to make practice approximate the real thing as closely as possible. I dusted off my hiking boots, which I hadn't worn in a couple of years.

We also needed ear protection. I had been using earplugs, since we didn't have any of those big earmuffs people use to muffle sound. But I had been warned that rifles are louder than shotguns, so I figured I'd use our noise-canceling headphones, since they had the same kind of fluffy ear surrounds as those earmuffs.

"You can't use those," Kevin said, taking them out of my hands as I was putting them in the bag.

"Why not?" I asked. "They're noise-canceling."

He pointed to the long curly cord (they were old-school). "What are you going to do with that?"

I considered. "I'll tuck it in my sweater."

"No."

I didn't see the problem, but he was pretty emphatic. I took the earplugs instead.

At the rifle range, there are benches where you set up your gun, and boards downrange to post targets on. When you're going out to hang or retrieve a target, everyone there agrees not to shoot for a while, and you walk out onto the range.

It didn't stop me from being a little apprehensive when we got there and walked out with our targets. It was weird walking out in front of a line of people with guns, even though every single one of them was pointing the muzzle in a safe direction.

Walking out, though, I felt a weird kind of drag on my right heel, like I had stepped on something that was trailing behind me. As I walked back, the whole damn boot sole came off, and I was flapping around like something out of *Mad* magazine.

When we got to the bench, I found that the heel had essentially rotted in half (salt air wreaks havoc in unexpected ways), and the bottom of the sole had separated from the rest of the boot.

This was unfortunate, because I was beginning to understand why Kevin had nixed the earphones. If there is any place on earth where you want to look competent and in control, it's the rifle range. Everyone there has loaded guns, and we all know our lives depend on our fellow shooters' ability to handle weapons safely. You simply do not want to look like an idiot.

Even though his nickname is Crash, and safety consciousness is generally not at the top of his priority list, Kevin makes an exception for guns. He is extremely careful, and emphasized to me the importance of gun-range etiquette. He was a little dismayed at the flapping sole, and when we got back to the bench, he pulled it off my boot. And then he pulled the other one off, just in case.

It was an inauspicious beginning.

I sat down on the bench and took a couple of minutes to stop feeling like an idiot. Then I loaded a slug and took aim. I carefully lined up the front and rear sights, and I tried to stay as still as possible. I squeezed the trigger, willing the slug to hit the target.

When the gun discharged, I was stunned. The noise was so loud and the recoil so strong that I felt as though I'd been physically assaulted. I was expecting something a bit louder than the standard-issue bang I was used to from shooting shells. But it wasn't even in the same ballpark.

Kevin thought I was hurt. "Are you okay?" he asked.

He had to ask twice before I told him I was fine, just really, really surprised. So surprised that—goddamnit!—I pointed the muzzle in an unsafe direction. In this case, at the guy sitting a few feet away, aiming his .22. My gun wasn't loaded, but that's not the point. Luckily, he didn't notice.

I just sat there for a while. The shot had set adrenaline flowing, and I needed to wait for it to dissipate before I tried again.

The good news was, I hit the target. By which I mean the piece of paper that had the target printed on it. I was a good six inches away from the center, where I'd been aiming. Six inches off at fifty yards isn't good.

Over the next couple of weeks, I got a little better, and when deer season actually opened, I had enough confidence to take a shot within forty yards or so. I knew going in that it was unlikely that such a thing would present itself, but Kevin increased our odds of venison by being comfortable out to almost a hundred yards.

What bothered me, going into that first season, wasn't the specter of deerlessness. It was that despite having taken hours of gun safety instruction, spent many afternoons practicing at the range, and shot one actual duck, guns still scared the bejeezus out of me.

The Four Seasons

You'd think that one of the advantages of hunting an overpopulated species is that they wouldn't be hard to find. Here on Cape Cod, though, where everybody and his dog hunts, I believe they've kept the herd down to an eco-friendly seven or eight. And that first season, literally every single hunter had more experience than we did, and was trying to find them.

As with real estate, the first three rules of deer hunting are location, location, location. If you are where the deer aren't, you're doomed to failure. You don't even get a chance to make those other mistakes, like smelling human or wearing blue.

Our chosen location was a town conservation area, a 180-acre parcel that I'd heard from reputable sources does have deer. Several weeks before the season started, Kevin and I cased the joint, hoping to find signs of them. I'd read up, and I knew to look for deer poop, spots on trees where bucks rub their antlers, bedding areas, and places in the terrain that deer were likely to funnel through.

Once you're in the woods, though, it all just looks like woods. We did spot several rubbed tree trunks and one pile of poop, but that was it. As for deer beds and deer funnels, I wouldn't have known them if they had road signs.

If you can't track deer, the next best thing is to track deer hunters. Okay, I missed the funnels, but even I found the pile of Bud Light cans under the tree stand.

That last bit is an exaggeration. Most hunters I know are safety- and wilderness-minded, and they don't drink and shoot or leave cans in their hunting grounds. But it's true that the best clue we got as to the deer's whereabouts came from evidence of hunters, rather than of deer.

We found a spot with the remains of a tree stand and figured that was as good as anything. We set up our deer blind, a pop-up tent big enough for two, in woodland camo, with openings through which you look for and shoot at your deer. It has little nylon leaves on the edges to help it blend in.

Maybe it's because my only exposure to camouflage as a child was in the cartoons, but I can't help thinking there's something inherently funny about it. Unless it's wartime and your camo is deadly serious, it's hard to glue leaves to your hat and make like a shrubbery without seeing the humor. It helps that our blind has a Laurel-and-Hardy tendency to spring uncontrollably into its popped-up position the moment you take it out of the bag. The thing makes me laugh every time.

The first morning of the season, before sunrise, we hiked out to it and set up shop. The weather was cold—about 25 degrees—but clear and still. We settled in and waited for 6:16, a half hour before sunrise, when the first shot could be fired.

Six-sixteen came and went. As did sunrise. As did an hour after sunrise. All we saw was the occasional hunter, who would spot our blind and wave his orange hat—the international sign for "Don't shoot me."

The two rules of deer blinds are no talking and no moving. As time went on and we didn't talk (much) or move (much), we became increasingly aware that it is all but impossible to keep your extremities warm while sitting still in subfreezing temperatures. The longer we sat, with zero evidence of deer, the more wildly unrealistic the idea of a deer became. I figured we'd see a yeti before we saw a deer.

It was a long, cold lesson in what things that aren't deer sound like. Squirrels, they don't sound like deer. Wind doesn't sound like deer. Sparrows don't sound like deer. But before you've heard an actual deer, they all sound like deer. I'd known to dress warmly, and I had more layers than a henhouse, but after two hours or so, I couldn't take it anymore. Luckily, neither could Kevin, who suggested we take a walk around. Not that we hoped to actually find a deer; we just needed some time out of the blind.

We took a little hike, half-heartedly scoped out some other potential sites, and returned to our blind for one last chance. By ten we were done.

After our first fruitless, deerless day, we changed the plan.

Cape Cod has a military base called the Massachusetts Military Reservation, a 22,000-acre tract just crawling with deer. The base is closed to civilians all year, opening for one week to allow hunters to cull their substantial white-tail herd.

You have to register in advance, which we'd done, and they let in up to five hundred hunters each day. Because the MMR used to be Otis Air Force Base, and everyone on Cape Cod still calls it that, this is always referred to as the Otis hunt.

Not all of the 22,000 acres are open. Since it's an active military base, there are areas with unexploded ordnance, clearly marked with scary signs and definitely off-limits. This should please any hunter committed to giving deer a sporting chance, as it creates vast safe havens. Although deer read only at a third-grade level and *ordnance* probably trips them up, they get the gist and go running for those areas at the first sound of guns.

That's what the only two deer we saw that morning were doing. Two bucks ran by about fifty yards from us, seeking refuge from the chaos that was descending on them. We didn't have a shot.

This was only my second day of deer hunting, but I was already coming to grips with the fact that the more I did this, the more I realized I had no clue about what I was doing.

Hunting is like fishing and even a little like gardening in that it doesn't lend itself to book learning. That doesn't mean there aren't books! There are many, many books. And each is one person's take, and they're all different. Not completely different, of course, and if you're starting from zero, I highly recommend reading some of them. I did, and it's not that I learned nothing. It's just that what I learned seemed to be of limited utility once I actually got out into the woods.

Lots of people hunt deer from blinds and tree stands, where you try and make sure the deer get in range before they notice you're there. But lots of people hunt by hiking through the woods, and as I hiked through the Otis woods I just couldn't fathom how that worked. The woods are filled with brush and dried leaves, and you can't walk anywhere without sounding like a herd of elephants. I could hear Kevin clearly at a hundred yards, so I figured the deer, who have very large ears and very good hearing, could hear us from Rhode Island.

Over the course of the morning, we saw lots of signs of deer—tracks, poop, and what I suspect were beds—but I had no hope of using these to help me figure out where the deer might be. When we went back to the clubhouse for lunch, we sat down with some of the guys who hunt

Otis every year, and I tried to cajole the secret of deer hunting out of them.

My cajoling skills probably need work. I sat down at a table with a bunch of strangers and said, "So, what's the secret of deer hunting?"

Oh, they laughed and they were friendly, but they didn't tell me the secret. Their gambit was to tell me there was no secret.

"Do you walk, or do you sit and wait?" Oh, a little bit of both.

"Which way gets you more deer?" Oh, it depends.

"How can you get a deer when you sound like a herd of elephants?" Oh, deer are curious.

Great.

That afternoon, we decided to go with sit and wait.

If you hang out with hunters, you're bound to hear it, more likely sooner than later: If you need to kill in order to have a successful hunt, you're not a hunter, you're a killer.

Being in the woods, the reasoning goes, is an end in itself. You learn the animal's habits and habitat. You learn how to make sense of the signs and the noises around you. You learn to appreciate tranquility, and the value of taking time off from civilization.

This is utter nonsense. What you really learn is how uncomfortable it is to sit in one spot for a very long time. You learn how adept deer are at giving you a wide berth. You learn that your own thoughts aren't such great company.

Normally, I use audiobooks to enliven tedious tasks (and there are a lot of them in my life). Give me a good book, and I can face just about anything. Hunting deer, though, you're supposed to be attuned to every noise. I tried an audiobook, at low volume, with only one ear plugged in, but it became clear that I wouldn't notice a deer until I took an antler in the gut.

So I was left to just think.

I cycled through everything I could think of to think about, and it was still only midafternoon. So I cycled through it again. I thought about the looming due date of the magazine article I wasn't working on. I thought about whether we really wanted to get two Scottish deerhounds. I thought about how to write about not shooting a deer in a way that was compelling and engaging. I wondered what Kevin was thinking.

All that took less than an hour, so I did some work on my all-purpose acceptance speech (Oscar, Pulitzer, Nobel, whatever), which I have to say is getting pretty good. I planned what I'd make for dinner. I figured out what I'd jury-rig to try to get the chickens to stop roosting on the nest box dividers. I developed some venison recipes, just in case. I wondered what problems Kevin was solving.

We packed it in a little after sunset, when there was just enough light to get us out of the woods. As we hiked back to the truck, Kevin said, "So, were you thinking about sex that whole time, too?"

"The whole time?"

"Sure," he said, as though it were the most natural thing in the world. And then paused. "Well, I also thought about that boat for a couple minutes." (We'd gone to look at one the day before.)

Although Kevin's version of not finding meaning sitting in the woods was obviously a bit different from mine, it was just as meaningless. Wendell Berry, we ain't.

My problem, I think, is that I am soulless. I don't look for meaning because I don't believe life has any beyond that with which we endow it with our words and deeds. I think the plants and animals in the woods are interesting, but I don't find mystery. My strategy for controlling anxiety is distraction, not contemplation, and sitting quietly with nothing to do doesn't clear my head. How can your head be clear when you know the bathtub needs scrubbing? Are the property taxes due? Is that a deer tick?

So in the many hours I spent in the woods in my first hunting season, there was no peace. There was no tranquility. And there sure as hell was no ten-point buck.

But there was a doe. A real live doe.

It was on the last day of the season, and our version of a hail-Mary hunt was going up to the Cape Cod National Seashore, a large preserve on the outer edge of the Cape. We picked a patch of woods and decided that I would stay put while Kevin hiked in a big circle, hoping to push any deer in the area in my general direction.

I was leaning on a tree, facing down the slope into a kind of bowl, watching and listening and trying not to think about stuff.

She came from my right, behind me. As soon as I heard the leaves rustle, I knew it was a deer, which was a little weird, given that I'd never heard one before. But it definitely wasn't like a squirrel or the wind or sparrows. The noise was a set of sharp, quick hoofsteps in the dry leaves. Clip . . . clip . . . clip clip.

The sound got closer and I slowly turned my head in her direction. There she was, maybe thirty yards away, crossing my field of vision across the ridge. She was easily in range, but there were two problems. First, I was facing down the slope, and to turn around and get a shot without spooking her would have been difficult. Second, she was right on the ridgeline, which meant I couldn't see what was on the other side of her. One of the cardinal rules of gun safety—right after pointing the muzzle in a safe direction—is to know what's beyond your target.

She went by behind me and headed down the slope and into the woods to my left. I had a shot. For someone of my minimal skill, it was a long shot, probably fifty yards. It was through trees and brambles, but I had a shot.

I pointed my gun. I saw her head and chest, looking very small above my gunsight. But it took me just a moment too long to line up the notch on the sight with the bead on the muzzle. It wasn't quite right, and I didn't have confidence in the shot.

I didn't take it. She went on her way, out of range.

That deer, though, stuck with me. And it was what got me out into the cold and the tedium, the ticks and the greenbrier, the next year. There will never be tranquility, but I was determined that there would, someday, be venison.

There wasn't, the next year, or even the two years after that, despite a multistate campaign that had us hitting up any friend in a deer-rich area for tips, lodging, and inevitably, consolation.

Before I met Kevin, I'd never heard the expression *on the schneid*. After I met Kevin, I heard it all the time. It means to be on a losing streak (*schneiden* means to cut in German), and Kevin went on the financial version of one almost from our first date. The U-turn in his trading success was so obvious that his friends started calling me "the schneid girl."

I didn't believe the trading schneid was my fault, but the deer schneid in part was. And Kevin's fault, too. Our lack of success hunting was to some extent undoubtedly due to our being overextended. We were doing so many things that it was hard to take the time that successful hunting requires. Hunters who bring home deer often start doing the legwork months in advance. They choose an area carefully and scout it thoroughly. They spend a lot of time in the field, understanding deer habits and behavior. And they do it year after year, getting better all the time.

Many years ago, I read biologist Edward O. Wilson's autobiography, *Naturalist*. When he was seven years old—seven!—he stood in the shallows of the Gulf of Mexico, watching a jellyfish, and he already knew what he was going to be when he grew up. He found his fascination early and never lost it; that is the mentality of a specialist.

I've always envied specialists and their mentality. I love the idea that you spend your whole life focused on a subject that captivates you, and you get really good at it. But I know that's not me, and it's not Kevin, either; we're generalists by nature. Our favorite thing to do is the thing we've never done before, and once we've done it three or four times, we're not thinking about fine-tuning our technique with a fifth or sixth iteration. We're looking for something new.

And that is the compensation for being a generalist. You get to do all kinds of stuff! But in this case we were trying to squeeze a little hunting in between running an oyster farm, raising livestock, keeping chickens, catching fish, and growing vegetables. It wasn't working.

In our defense, I will point out that all those specialist-mentality hunters doing all that legwork have made it tough on us generalist-mentality newcomers. Years of hunting, all over the Northeast, have culled all the stupid, slow, or friendly deer, leaving only the streetwise, fast, suspicious ones. It is those deer that survive into their deery dot-age, reproducing and volunteering their time to teach Hunter Evasion classes to the youngsters.

It was obviously working.

It took us four whole years to figure out that if we wanted to shoot a deer, we'd have to do something different. That's why, in season five, we went to Gene's house, in Virginia.

Gene is our friend because of sea salt. When I wrote a piece about making it for *The Washington Post*, I got an actual handwritten letter from him in response. Although Gene has a farm in Virginia, he's a part-time Cape Codder, and he'd always wondered about the process. So the next time he was in our neck of the woods, we got together and showed him.

Since then, he and his wife, Polly, have become our dear friends. And they happen to have a large farm—some fields, some woods—that they both assured us is home to many, many deer.

We showed up the day before the season opened, to get a feel for the place. Gene had given us very specific directions and warned that we should go slowly on his half-mile-long driveway. "There may be deer on it."

Yeah, right. Deer on the driveway. Hanging with the yeti.

We turned into his driveway, and there must have been twenty of them.

"There's deer in the driveway," I said in absolute astonishment. We stopped the truck and watched them saunter, unconcerned, off to the left and into the woods. It was more deer than we had seen in all four fruitless hunting seasons. Surely, with so many deer . . .

We spent that afternoon walking the property, looking for deery spots. And we saw deer, or signs of deer, just about everywhere. The farm is a 300-acre sardine can of deer. You can practically shoot at random and hit one.

Kevin and I each picked a field and set up makeshift blinds; his was a hay bale, mine was the truck bed (deer were used to seeing trucks around the place). That evening—the day before the season opened— we both sat in our spots to get a deer preview.

In my field, at first there were no deer. A bit later, there were still no deer. And then, suddenly, there were deer. I didn't hear them arrive, I just saw that a few brown-gray spots, suspiciously different from the brown-gray background, were moving. It was as though they had just seeped out of the woods. Once I was attuned to what a deer at dusk looks like, I saw that there were at least a dozen. Maybe two.

Kevin, in his field, saw even more than I did.

Surely, with so many deer . . .

The next morning, predawn, Kevin went to his hay bale and I climbed into the truck bed. At first light, I could just barely make out deer, but they kept their distance. There were at least six or eight, but not the Mongol hordes of the evening before. I watched them, willing them to come closer. But as the sky brightened, they dispersed, and a mere fifteen minutes after sunrise they were gone. It's like they knew. I decided to try something else.

The something else was another cleared area, upland of a little pond, bordered by some tall grass. I had barely settled in the grass, behind a pretty significant rock, when two small does came up the hill right toward me. I was surprised that they didn't seem to know I was there, and almost without warning, the lead doe was a mere ten yards away.

I pointed the gun. I had a shot. But it didn't feel right. I hadn't had time to find a position that felt solid, with my gun steady. I felt rushed and unready. I didn't take the shot. The does turned tail when I moved and trotted down the hill.

This was, to date, the closest encounter with deer I'd had, and it surprised me that merely having one clear in my sights and thinking about shooting it was enough to set the adrenaline flowing.

I found a comfortable position and waited for my heart rate to go down. Once it did, I positioned my gun on the rock, with my scarf as a pad. There were a few deer in the distance, but they wandered into the woods. I sat alone, deerless, for probably twenty minutes. And then two small deer appeared on my left, moving toward me. They slowly came into range, stopping to graze, stopping to listen, then taking a few steps. After about ten minutes, the closer of the two, a button buck, wasn't more than fifteen yards away, but he was facing me. I needed him to turn broadside. For a long time, he didn't. I kept my gun trained and tried to breathe, slowly and calmly.

Deer hunting, in my imagination, happened fast. You sit in your blind, the deer shows up, and either you have a shot or you don't. In real life, I had plenty of time. Time to aim, to think, to decide. When he turned, I was ready. I aimed for just behind his shoulder, a little below the center of the body. For the first time in my life, I took a shot at a deer.

He was close enough that I saw the red bloom on his side. The shot was, astonishingly, perfect.

Guns are funny that way. They fire where you aim them, particularly at short range. It's very reassuring.

The little buck jumped and promptly ran into the woods, about ten

---

yards away, and I did what everyone tells you to do in that situation, which is, for a minute, nothing. Take a breath. Empty the gun. Let the adrenaline subside.

I had carefully noted where he ran into the woods, a skill I've honed from years of playing the kind of golf game in which things go into the woods all the time. What I dreaded—what every hunter dreads—is wounding an animal and not being able to track it. I dreaded it, but I didn't think it was likely. I saw the shot, and although I knew precious little about deer hunting, I did know it was the kind of shot that kills.

The deer wasn't more than ten yards in, dead under a tree. It was very small. But it was a deer, and I had shot it. I had shot it carefully and well. I dragged the little buck back out into the field to gut it.

I had, at this point in my killing career, gutted many, many birds, but only a few mammals, and a couple rabbits and a raccoon don't really prepare you for a deer. The principle is the same, though. The insides of an animal are all connected, and if you release the top (the trachea and esophagus) and the bottom (the rectum), and open the belly, you can pull them all out in a heap.

Someone experienced can do this to a deer carcass in just a few minutes. When you do it yourself, for the first time, it takes half the morning. You will take so many tentative strokes that the deer's fur will dull your knife. You will be unsure what is bowel and what is fascia. Just when you think you've got it all, you will find yet another obscure place where the insides are connected to the body cavity.

But you'll get there.

I dragged the cleaned carcass down to the house.

Although much of my career has been characterized by underachievement, there have been a handful of accomplishments I've been proud of. I've written a few useful things and even won an award or two. I can fillet a bluefish perfectly and make a world-class pecan pie. On a good day, I can do twenty push-ups. Although some of those things are obviously more important than others, I'd use *pride* to describe all of them.

The deer was an accomplishment of a different order. I took it to the local processor, and I felt a brain-stem level of satisfaction, walking in with blood on my boots, my deer in the truck. Man, the hunter. Except, woman.

There was a kid, probably not out of his teens, working on the carcass of a large buck, and I asked him if they could take my deer. Sure they could, and he walked out with me to get it. I opened the tailgate, and there was my little buck, on a tarp. My little buck, first deer of my life. My little buck, shot perfectly.

The kid took a look at it. Of course I didn't expect him to be impressed, when I had pulled him away from an eight-point behemoth.

"Um," the kid said. "Nice truck."

The truck was the 2008 Ford F-250 diesel that we'd bought when we got our bigger boat, and it is indeed a nice truck. It is far and away the best truck we have ever owned. The truck, compared to other trucks, was much better than the deer, compared to other deer. It took a little of the wind out of my sails.

The kid picked the deer up off the tarp, effortlessly, and we walked inside to do the paperwork.

"I know it's small," I couldn't help saying, "but it's the first deer I ever shot."

He put the pen down. "Really?" He looked at me a bit more closely. I assume he'd been hunting since single digits, and a middle-aged woman who just shot her first deer was something of a curiosity.

And then he smiled. "Congratulations," he said. "Looks like your shot was just right." He pointed to the red spot on the deer's hide.

I find it hard to describe feelings. You can't re-create them at will, and a memory of a feeling is a pallid and lackluster thing. But that day I did something I wasn't sure I had in me, and it felt remarkable.

Kevin, it turned out, shot a much larger deer while I was gone, so we headed home with some sixty pounds of venison. Since then, we've been back several times, and we come home with deer every time. But this is only because Gene and Polly's farm is a place where you can get a deer without being a hunter. I'm just a harvester; there's no skill involved.

Before our second trip, I bought a rifle, which considerably expanded my range. I've shot a half dozen deer over the years, and I'm happy to report that each has dropped with one shot. That's not a testament to my marksmanship, though. Guns shoot where you aim them, and all you have to be is careful. And have access to a 300-acre sardine can of deer.

From that first trip to this day, we have always had venison in the freezer.

It makes a nice dinner, but it's also a bridge-builder. All our first-hand food activities have connected us to our community and introduced us to people we wouldn't have met otherwise, but none as much as hunting. I'm a left-leaning centrist with a libertarian streak, and the hunting world most definitely leans right. Meeting people who don't share your politics, outside the realm of politics, gives you a chance to see them as three-dimensional, as people who share an interest with you, as people you might even like.

In a polarized world, I think that's a good thing, and it has made my life richer. In my day job, as a *Washington Post* columnist, I often find myself talking with farmers who come from rural, mostly right-leaning, church-oriented communities. Sometimes that happens in the middle of a cornfield. I can understand that they might be wary when they've invited a journalist who writes for a paper in a coastal, left-leaning city to their farm. But most of them hunt or come from hunting families or have problems with deer on their farms, or all three. So we can talk about hunting. I can show them the picture of the last deer I shot, at which point they'll take out their phone and show me theirs.

If we can talk about hunting, we can talk about guns. And if we can talk about guns, we can talk about anything. Once we get to those other things, we're a little more comfortable with each other, which makes it easier both to talk and to listen.

I don't tell them that I still hate guns, and despite years of practice and my very best intentions, I occasionally point the muzzle in an unsafe direction.

HOW TO BE A HARVESTER

Deer hunting is hard; it takes skill and practice. But there are a lot of corners you can cut if, like me, you just want to stock the freezer.

- **Find your spot.** This is everything. If you're consigned to hunt where the deer are elusive and wary, you have to be a real hunter. But if you can find a place that's deer-rich, you can be a harvester. Although there are some public lands that fill the bill, private land is probably your best bet. And you don't necessarily need a farm; lots of people live in areas where deer wander into the backyard and hunting is permitted. Ask nicely.

- **Get a gun that fits you, one you're comfortable with.** A rifle with a scope is the best tool for this job. If you're using a scope, make sure it's sighted in properly (so the scope is correctly aligned with the rifle barrel). And practice. To shoot a deer in a deery place, you don't have to spend years developing hunter skills, but gun safety and handling is not a corner you can cut.

- **Consider bowhunting.** There are lots of places overrun with deer that are also overrun with people, and you're probably not allowed to use a gun. Bows are allowed in many places where guns aren't.

(continued)

- **If you can, shoot from a place where deer are used to seeing humans.** If you go out in the woods where humans usually aren't, you have to figure out how to make the deer not notice you (cover up your smell, go up in a tree stand, be very quiet). But if you're in a place where humans usually are, your presence will be unremarkable.

- **Remember that you're in it for meat, not bragging rights.** Take the deer you can shoot with confidence, without regard for the antlers. Do what you can to make it easier, including shooting a deer over bait, if that's legal where you're hunting. Real hunters will sneer, but if you're hunting for the table, anything that helps ensure you will have a clean kill is good.

- **Know the rules, which vary state by state.** Follow the rules. Hunters who don't give all hunters a bad name.

And I know I don't have to tell you this, but always point the muzzle in a safe direction.

DINNER, WHICH IS THE POINT

K evin and I got married in 2004. Our wedding was low-key, just us and our two oldest friends at Manhattan's City Hall on a Tuesday morning. Then breakfast at the Mercer Kitchen in SoHo, and off to Arizona for five days of golf school.

When we came home—tanned, rested, and with a renewed emphasis on our short game—I found my wedding gift. There in my kitchen, wrapped up with a giant bow on top, was a brand-new Viking stove.

The stove I'd been cooking on for close to a decade was, not to put too fine a point on it, a piece of shit. I didn't realize just how bad it was until one day I accidentally let a pot of beans boil over. I cleaned up the stovetop and thought I was done until I noticed the puddle on the floor. The bean liquid had found a path all the way through the stove to collect next to the right front leg.

I was fine with it. I figure if you can cook, you can cook on anything. Give me a heat source—any heat source—and I'll make you dinner. But I did think it would be nice to have a better stove, with a hotter hot and a lower simmer. And Kevin, who has a constitutional aversion to the crappy version of anything, wanted to replace it from the day he moved in. The problem was, it was only twenty-four inches wide, and there weren't any decent stoves that size.

Except for just the one. The Viking. Which my husband bought on the sly and had installed while we were gone.

Perhaps not every woman would appreciate a stove as a wedding present, the implication being that she would spend her married life tethered to it, but I actually shed tears. I couldn't have imagined a better gift.

You might be wondering what I got him. I'm sorry to report that it never occurred to me that one's own wedding was a gift-giving occasion. Now that I'm twenty years in, I can tell you that it's a good leading indicator when your husband not only gives you a Viking stove for your wedding but doesn't resent it when you give him nothing at all.

When we moved to the Cape, I had to leave my Viking behind, and I was back to cooking on the same kind of crappy stove I'd been cooking on all my life. And I was fine with it. If you can cook, you can cook on anything.

But, again, I wanted something better. We were spending an ungodly amount of time and effort procuring food, and I wanted a way to cook it that was in the spirit of the thing. Sure, we could have just bought a better stove (eventually we did). But where's the fun in that? We have land! We have wood! And we have a track record of taking on projects for which we have no relevant experience.

A wood-fired oven was called for.

It was definitely in the spirit of the thing. If we were going to glean dinner from the landscape, let's cook it outside and feed it to our friends. Preferably on pizza.

We'd been perfecting our pizza for a couple years. We had dialed in an excellent recipe, using King Arthur high-protein flour, but there's a limit to how good you can get with a pizza stone in our crappy old oven. The best pizza—with the char on the bottom, the elasticity in the crust, the cooked-through topping—requires high heat. And what better vehicle for your first-hand tomatoes, basil, wild mushrooms, and venison?

The important part of a wood-fired oven is the igloo that forms its heart. It has to be the right shape to get the air to flow; getting it wrong means a nonfunctioning oven. Because it was tricky, we were thinking about buying that part—a number of companies sell them—and just building the insulated housing around it. But we were choking on the price tag; the one we liked, made by a company called Fogazzo, was $2,699.

Then we found a book called *Build Your Own Earth Oven*, by Kiko Denzer. This book has been in print almost since there have been ovens, because there is a never-ending appetite for building them out of mud.

Literally, mud. The stuff the ground is made of. Clay, soil, even Carver coarse sand—if you can walk on it, you can build an oven with it. Denzer tells you how, with detailed instructions and copious illustrations. And all you need is a weekend, a can-do attitude, and maybe a hundred bucks. It's the kind of project that has Tamar and Kevin written all over it.

But I was a little suspicious. Could that possibly work? Can we get the shape right? Will the air flow properly? Could you really build something out of mud that can reasonably stand in for something that costs $2,699? But people have been building ovens for millennia, and they didn't call 1-866-FOGAZZO. If it was good enough for the Sumerians, it's good enough for us. Besides, if it doesn't work, we can tear it down, return it to the earth whence it came, and pick up the phone.

Rock On

Before you build an oven, you have to build the pedestal it's going to sit on. There are lots of makeshift options, and Denzer is a man after our own hearts in the makeshift department. Use washing machines, he suggests. Or five-gallon buckets filled with cement, railroad ties, or tires filled with sand.

Or you can build a foundation out of stones. Because we wanted ours to weather Cape Cod winters for a good long time, and we had already used up our lifetime allotment of repurposed washing machines, that's what we went with.

And it was my job.

I am the rock-stacker in the family for the same reason I am the animal-breaker-downer: Kevin has neither the patience nor the inclination. When we put a French drain (which isn't nearly as sexy as other French things) in our outdoor shower, I actually enjoyed piecing together the stone jigsaw puzzle that became the shower floor. There's something about taking a pile of irregular stones and imposing order on them that calls to me.

The problem is that irregular stones don't care to have order imposed on them. While stones have many fine qualities—attractiveness and durability come to mind—flexibility is not their long suit. It is very difficult to get them to play nice with other stones, if they are not so inclined.

Oh sure, it started off pretty well. I used big, flat stones that stacked well and looked good. Unfortunately, as the walls got higher, the job got harder, both because I was working with an increasingly irregular surface and because I was running out of good stones. The thing was over two feet high when I realized it just wasn't going to work.

Which reminded me of one of my all-time favorite jokes:

Q. What do you get when you cross a mobster with a deconstructionist?
A. Someone who makes you an offer you can't understand.

I've always thought deconstruction, the literary theory, was hogwash. But it's way better than literal deconstruction. It was like the time I had to dig up all my sunchokes, only heavier. The work you do to undo the work you did wrong is the worst work there is.

So I called Rick. You may remember him for his dramatic reenactment of that time Blondie shat all over Kevin, but he is more than a mere thespian. He's a stone guy. He reads about stones, he thinks about stones, he scours the countryside for wayward stones and takes them home to install in the landscape around his house.

He came over to assess the situation.

The first thing he said was "You're going to need more stones."

"MORE stones?" I whined piteously. I had two pallets and, more to the point, $500 of stones already.

"You don't use them all," Rick said. "So you need more than you think."

So not only would I have to buy more stones, I could look forward to a large pile of leftover, incorrigibly irregular stones, good for nothing. Rick saved me from this fate by giving me some from his collection. It was only three or four, but because they were big, they displaced many smaller stones. Rick also showed me how large and small stones look good together and gave me some stacking tips.

My second version was a definite improvement over the first, but all I could see was the awkward spots. I seriously considered taking it down and trying a third time, but come on. When you tackle a job that you've never done before, one that skilled craftsmen spend years learning, you can't go into it thinking your stone wall will look like their stone wall. I needed to downgrade my expectations from "beautiful" to "serviceable."

And serviceable it was, solid and straight. Yes, there were some dodgy areas, but there were other parts that were downright harmonious. Kevin was actually impressed and thought it would be nuts to tear it down. So I didn't, and we moved on to the oven-building portion of the program.

Oven-Ready

At this point we were a year and nearly a thousand bucks into our weekend project, and all we'd done was build a pedestal. The only progress we'd made on the oven itself was to take samples of earth from various spots to see which might make the best dome-building material.

And if Home Depot had carried firebricks, we might actually have built that dome.

Firebricks look like ordinary bricks, but are engineered to withstand high heat, and we needed them for the base of the oven. But because garden-variety home-improvement stores in our area don't carry them, we had to venture to a specialty store called Drywall Masonry Supplies, which is where our well-laid plans got completely derailed. I blame Kristen, whose family owns the store and who was behind the counter when we showed up.

There are good things and bad things about living in a small town. On the minus side, you will encounter petty bureaucrats exacting obeisance for playing in their fiefdom. When you try to find preserved lemons, people will keep trying to sell you lemon preserves. The odds of running into people you know around town are high, so you should probably put on a bra before you go to the supermarket.

But the plus side is everywhere, and heartwarming. When we lost a trailer wheel and dropped our boat on a main road, the flatbed driver who picked it up turned out to be a neighbor. He knew our lake and figured out how to launch the boat from his flatbed, so he could deliver the trailer, empty, to our house for repairs. And he didn't charge extra.

The local car repair shop, Moore Automotive, didn't charge, either, when they figured out the reason my car, which has a manual transmission, was mysteriously frozen in first gear. They simply removed the oyster shell, which a rat had taken from our driveway and dropped in the gearshift linkage, and added the story to their list of uniquely Cape Cod automobile mishaps.

And then there are little serendipitous pleasures, like going to the pub on live-music night and discovering that your plumber is the lead singer in the AC/DC cover band, and he's not half bad. As we've become more closely connected with our community, there have been a lot of those.

I walked into Drywall Masonry Supplies with some trepidation. I figured they were used to working with builders and contractors, who know what they need and buy things in industrial quantities. I wasn't sure how they'd take to two amateurs trying to build a wood-fired oven, but Kristen was all over it.

Not only did she tell us everything we needed to know about fire-brick, she made a phone call to a local mason who had built a wood-fired oven to ask if he had any tips. He invited us over to see his creation, and the moment Kevin saw his beautiful brick dome, Kiko Denzer was out of the loop. Our oven would have to be brick.

It's a good thing we already knew Kristen, because we had to go back to her for castable refractory mortar, fireclay, and masonry cement. And a lot more bricks.

It was only after we bought the supplies that Kevin discovered that dome-building was the very apex of masonry proficiency. Once you spend an entire career building simple square things out of brick, then maybe—maybe—you can tackle a dome.

As months ticked by and Kevin's progress was limited to watching many, many dome-building videos, I pointed out that we could go back to Plan A, which was the Fogazzo $2,699 oven insert. We had a serviceable base for it.

He wasn't ready to capitulate, particularly not to the tune of $2,699. But he also wasn't ready to build the dome, so we remained in our wood-fired purgatory, waiting for the solution to present itself.

And then for a fleeting moment, I thought it did. We were driving in one of the posher parts of Cape Cod and passed a big, beautiful house with a yard sale going on. And there on the ground, clearly for sale, was an igloo-shaped oven insert. I could hardly believe it.

"Did you see that??!" I said to Kevin, who was driving.

Of course he'd seen it. He has bionic peripheral vision. But he didn't seem excited.

"They must have started building an oven and changed their mind," I said. But he didn't slow down or give any indication that he was planning to turn around.

"Don't you think we should at least look at it?" I couldn't understand his reluctance.

"Honey," he said gently, "that was a doghouse."

I don't know whether this incident was what spurred Kevin on to action or whether it was just a coincidence, but the very next week, which was more than two years after we first began this project, he started the dome.

I watched as he laid his soldier course—the first tier of bricks, which stand on their short end—and then layered tier after tier, each smaller than the tier before, supported by a scaffold of bamboo.

He laid out the space for the door, which is supposed to be 63 percent of the height of the dome, and built the bricks around the entryway. When it was all finished, he cut a keystone for the very top, and it was done.

After we admired it for a couple days, we insulated it with a ceramic fiber blanket and encased it in a layer of the refractory concrete, specially formulated for high-heat applications, that we'd gotten from Kristen. We carved a little heart with "KF+TH" in the back.

Before we invited people over for pizza, we fired it up to make sure it did what it was supposed to do. And it did! The air circulated. The heat maxed out our infrared thermometer, which can measure up to 932 degrees. Nothing cracked.

We invited friends, and two years and nine months after we broke ground on our wood-fired oven, Kevin pulled the first pizza out of it. It was the first of many pizzas at many parties, and the days when we have the oven lit and our friends scattered around our deck are some of the best I know. There is a primordial, a reptilian, a deep-seated satisfaction in taking food we harvested, cooking it in an oven we built, and feeding it to people we love.

Our menus are a direct reflection of those people, the community we've become a part of. There's smoked bluefish spread on every table, so Amy and Bob are there even when they're not. The tomatoes in the sauce come from plants Christl gave us as seedlings. There wouldn't be venison meatballs without Gene and an invitation to his farm in Virginia. The turkey sausage connects us to Sam and the many people, both friends and strangers, who have worked side by side with us to turn animals into food as carefully and responsibly as we can. And the oven itself rests on Rick's rocks.

Although Euell Gibbons isn't a personal friend, and is also dead, he's there in the dandelion wine we break out when we're sure everyone is having a good enough time to think it's delicious.

Why, Again?

We started this whole enterprise of getting our food first-hand as something more than a lark, but not much more. It was supposed to be a fun project where we ate one food a day that we hunted or fished, gathered or grew. It ended up being so compelling that we built a stone monument to it. To think that, just a few years before, I thought putting some tomato plants in a whiskey barrel was stretching my limits.

But that's the thing about stretching your limits; every time you do it, you have a new limit to stretch. The whiskey barrels set me up for the full-fledged garden, which made the backyard chickens seem like a natural extension. And if you've got chickens, surely you can have turkeys. And if you kill the turkeys, maybe you can kill a deer, too. By then it makes perfect sense that you can take huge piles of stone and brick and turn them into an oven to cook all those things. I learned how to garden and forage, to fish and to hunt. But mostly I learned how to do.

It is the doing, even more than the food, that ties all these activities together. What makes first-hand food powerful is the investment, the first-handedness, and I have been surprised by that power since that very first tomato.

When we began, I couldn't quite put my finger on the source of that power, and I didn't have a good answer when people asked me the most basic question about our project: Why?

Many of the people doing the kinds of things we do are trying for self-sufficiency, but we definitely weren't. On a logistical level, it requires more work than I'm willing to do; the year I kept track, we got only about 30 percent of our calories from first-hand food, despite spending an unconscionable amount of time procuring it. But I'm not on board with it ideologically, either. Interdependence is, I think, part of what makes us civilized. I do love a good pioneer spirit, but self-sufficiency implies keeping your fellow man at arm's length. In a way, it's a vote of nonparticipation.

Yet learning to rely on ourselves to solve problems, rather than referring them to people who had solved them before, was the essence of our undertaking. The difference between self-sufficiency and self-reliance is, I think, the goal. Self-sufficiency is about your relationship to the wider world. Self-reliance is just about you. You, getting out of your armchair and doing.

The combination of Cape Cod and Kevin tapped into my inner doer, which had been fully dormant but, according to my mother, had been there from the very moment I could express myself. To hear her tell it, I was a stubborn, obnoxious baby (she didn't use those exact words), bent on having my own way. Mom decided that in the interest of peace, she would give me as much autonomy as it was possible to give to a child who couldn't walk yet. And so it was, one morning when I was eight or nine months old, when I said my first word. (I was a precocious talker, but I made up for it by being behind the curve in every other area of development.)

My mother was trying to dress me, and I was having none of it. I squirmed and fought and finally, my patience at an end, snatched the clothes away. "Self!" I proclaimed. I got my pants on my head, but, god-damnit, I was going to dress myself.

I was bent on self-reliance at the ripe old age of zero, but somewhere along the way the armchair won out.

As I write this, it's been twelve years of gardening and gathering, fishing and hunting. Twelve years of building, and sometimes rebuilding. Of improvising and problem-solving. Of a distinct overreliance on the seat of our pants. Twelve years of launching into project after project.

And it has been the opposite of self-sufficient. Doing it has made Kevin and me more interdependent, not less. It has connected us to the first-hand food community, which is broad and deep and diverse. It's bound together by the evolutionary imperative to feed ourselves and our family, and I have never talked to anyone who participates who doesn't feel the difference between the food you buy and the food you grow or hunt or raise.

I feel that difference every time I go to the grocery store. The stuff in the boxes and bags doesn't even seem like food to me anymore. Don't get me wrong—not everything in a box or a bag is bad for you. But too many of those boxes and bags are filled with food specifically engineered to override your best judgment with sugar, salt, fat, and flavor, so it's not surprising we find them irresistible. You still can't leave me alone with a bag of Doritos. But I've internalized the idea that food is something different from that. Food comes from plants and animals that are very real to me, and that's what I put on our dinner table.

It's about more than food, though. At least for me. Every time you solve a problem, it builds you up a little bit. It can be a small problem like designing a brooder or keeping the slugs out of the mushrooms, or a bigger problem like improving your diet or reaching your goal weight.

It was a few years back when the Japanese organizing expert Marie Kondo wrote an international bestseller making the case that tidying up could be life-changing, and I got the book to see what all the fuss was about. After tidying up, Kondo claims, some of her clients were finally able to lose weight or get fit or launch their own business or get that long-overdue divorce.

Yeah, right, I thought. But then I thought again. The exact same thing was happening to me. Each problem Kevin and I solved put wind in my sails and made it that much easier to take on the next one. Kondo's clients didn't change their lives because they had a clean house. They changed their lives because solving a problem that's in your control changes you.

Our food culture hasn't given us a lot of leeway to solve problems for ourselves; we've been fed a steady diet of disempowerment in the form of both foods and ideas that appeal to our worst instincts. The food's obvious: boxes and bags of calorie-dense, nutrition-free stuff designed to tempt us into overeating. But the ideas are just as insidious. Just do exactly what I tell you, diet experts say, and you'll feel better and lose weight.

How's that working out for us as a society?

The food you grow or forage or hunt appeals to the best in you. The you who's willing to give it a whirl. The you who takes dinner into your own hands. The you who gets out of your armchair.

We ate, and I logged, at least one first-hand food every day for several years, but then it just became part of how we eat. I still miss New York, but I can't imagine giving up everything we do on Cape Cod. I want to continue to be able to walk out to the chicken coop and get our breakfast.

Until we came here, I'd spent my entire adult life understanding things by reading, thinking, and talking—armchair activities all. But going outside, getting dirty, and coming home with food has a different kind of persuasive power. Things that don't come easy—eating better, even being better—can start to happen, almost of their own accord, as experience changes the way you see the world. You will at some point undoubtedly get your pants on your head. But that's just the next problem to solve.

Start small. Go mushroom-hunting. Build a raised bed. Plant an herb garden and see if it speaks to you.

Besides, what's the downside? Basil?

AUTHOR'S NOTE

Thanks for coming to spend time with Kevin and me. I hope you enjoyed your trip to our neck of the woods.

Just a couple of notes about the story. For starters, bits and pieces of it have been published elsewhere, so if you come across a paragraph or a joke or a story that sounds familiar, that's probably why. I've also used a lot of material from the blog I wrote as we were doing all these things.

I've taken some liberties with the timeline and sometimes compressed a couple of events into one, so I didn't have to keep shuttling you back and forth to projects or activities. I've also changed some of the names and places to safeguard privacy (although all fishing spots are legit). Conversations are not guaranteed to be verbatim; sometimes I've included what Kevin and I *wish* we'd said. This is one of the great perks of writing a book.

Also, Kevin still disputes some aspects of the chicken plucker story.

Other than that, the book is a pretty close approximation of what really happens around here, and I've got the chicken coop, wood-fired oven, lobster traps, raised beds, turkey pen, boats, trucks, and trailers to prove it.

ACKNOWLEDGMENTS

First and last, there is my husband, Kevin Flaherty. Without him and his twenty years of horizon-widening, this book wouldn't exist and, more important, neither would the version of me who wrote it. Besides, every writer should be married to someone who's such good material.

Then there are the many, many food people. Some are in the book by name, but all are in the book in spirit. I am grateful to everyone who helped me figure out gardening and fishing, hunting and gathering. And my neighbors have tolerated all kinds of livestock-related shenanigans without complaining even once.

And where would I be without my friends who write, who have gotten me through this and other projects? Thanks to a long list of them who have helped me navigate the world of books and articles and agents and publishers and just plain writing: Cathy Barrow, Bonnie Benwick, Ruth DeFries, Miriam Horn, Dianne and Doug Langeland, Alan Levinovitz, Amanda Little, Rachel Laudan, Charles Mann, Jill Melton, Katie Rogin, Mark Schatzker, Meera Subramanian, and Robyn Surprenant.

Particular thanks to Michael Easter, who introduced me to agents Steve Troha and Jan Baumer, of Folio Literary Management. They brought top-tier professionalism and unfailing enthusiasm to the project, and went on to sell it to the kind of editor writers dream about. Michelle Howry at Putnam can cut huge chunks of your prose but somehow manage to make you feel good about it. She took a story and shaped it into a book.

Getting that book to the point where it can see the light of day takes a lot of people, and I hit the jackpot with the teams at Folio and Putnam. I couldn't have asked for smarter, nicer, more supportive people in my corner.

Joe Yonan, my editor at *The Washington Post*, gave me the latitude to explore some of the book's ideas in my column, but the oversight to make sure I didn't say anything stupid. Todd and Beth Marcus have always been there with moral, titular, and photographic support, as well as a never-ending supply of Cape Cod Beer. My mom, Barbara Haspel, has read and reread more of my work than any mortal should have to, and laughed at every joke, every time.

And first and last, there is Kevin.

INDEX

humane treatment of animals
and conventionally raised meats, 194
and fishing for food vs. sport, 107–8
and minimizing suffering, 194
and misconceptions about taste of
foods, 66–67
as priority, 107–8, 194
and slaughtering practices,
175–78, 182
Hunter Angler Gardener Cook
website, 138
hunting, 189–99
and antlers/trophies, 218
birds, 197, 199
blinds used in, 205
books about, 206
as bridge-builder, 216–17
challenges of, 207–9
and eating overpopulated animals,
193, 194
encounters with deer, 209–10, 213
and ethos of hunters, 207
and gutting deer, 214
harvester model of, 216, 217–18
and Hunter Safety class, 195–96
importance of location, 203–4, 217, 218
and living in rural areas, 192
and preparations of successful hunters,
210–11
and prey/not-prey categories of
animals, 192–93
satisfaction from, 215
as source of first-hand food, 216
successful season in, 211–16
unsuccessful attempts at, 203–11
See also guns

I
Iberian ham, 133
ice fishing, 78–82
insects
and chickens, 68
and fig tree, 22, 25, 26
and first-year gardens, 14
in food, 143, 146–47
and insecticides, 22, 23–25
and perennial greens, 19

interdependence, xxi, 228, 229
Iverson, Jean, 7

J
Jake Principle, 17–18, 82
Japanese eggplant, 15
Jerusalem artichokes, 19–20
Jonah crabs, 104
junk/processed foods, 35, 229–30

K
Kelly Farm, 7
Kevin (husband)
background of, 60–61
and boat purchase, 78, 83–85
building skills of, 154–55
and chicken coop, 46, 47–51, 54–57
and chickens, 59–61
and Competent Spouse Doctrine,
54, 154
"Crash" nickname, 189, 190, 191, 202
as doer, xii
early relationship with, xii
and feather pluckers, 170–73, 174–75,
178–79, 182
full-throttle tendencies of, 189–90
guns of, 190–91
hunting deer, 216
peripheral vision of, 141–42, 226
previous life in commodity trading,
xviii, 141, 189
problem-solving of, 44–45
as risk-taker, 189–90
and rooftop garden, xiii–xviii
shooting skills of, 197
and Viking stove, 219–20
Kondo, Marie, 230

L
"The Learning Curve" (Gawande),
114–15
learning from experience, 93
leeks
ease and economy of, 34
foraging for, 149
lettuces, 15
liberty vs. security of animals, 71